1-99

UXBRIDGE
PAST

First published 1994
by Historical Publications Ltd
32 Ellington Street, London N7 8PL
(Telephone 071-607 1628)

ISBN 0 948667 30 3
British Library Cataloguing-in-Publication Data.
A catalogue record for this book is available from the British Library

Typeset by Historical Publications Ltd
Printed in Zaragoza, Spain by
Edelvives

UXBRIDGE PAST

A Visual History

by Carolynne Cotton

HISTORICAL PUBLICATIONS

Acknowledgments

I should like to acknowledge the help and forbearance shown by my colleagues at Hillingdon Libraries, in particular the fellow members of the Heritage Service and the Information Technology Team.

My grateful thanks go to Miss Mary Pearce FLA, former Local History Librarian and Archivist of Hillingdon, and Philip Colehan, former Borough Librarian, without whose help and advice the original work for this book would never have been completed.

Ken Pearce, Chairman of the Uxbridge Local History and Archives Society, has kept me on the right track, but any mistakes are purely mine!

Last, by not least, thanks to my family; my husband Jonathan and son Christopher, for their unfailing support.

The Illustrations

Other than those noted below, the illustrations are reproduced with the permission of Hillingdon Heritage Services. Others are reproduced with the kind permission of the following:

A. Bell: *177, 178, 179, 184, 185*
Bodleian Library: *6*
Museum of London: *1*
Uxbridge Gazette: *150, 151, 154, 156, 157, 158, 160, 162, 164, 166, 167, 168, 169, 172*
B. Williams: *183*

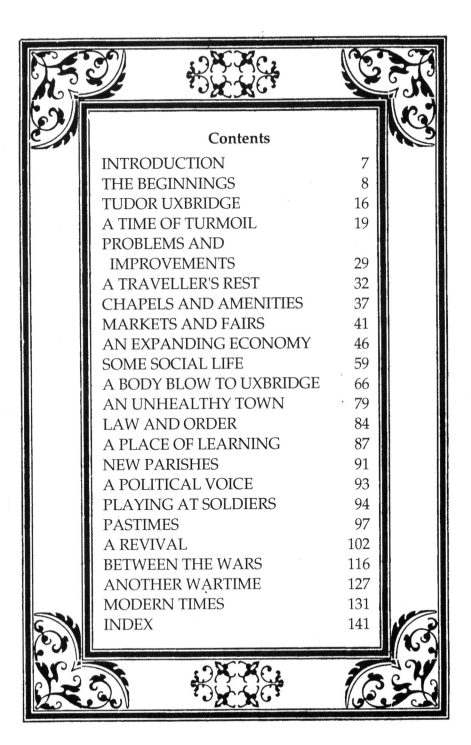

Contents

Further Reading

BLAKE, J.   *A Study of the growth and changes of industry related to improvements in communications in the Uxbridge area* (ms. 1979).

CATTLE, J.T.   *The fight for Uxbridge's market tolls* (ms. 1939).

CHAMBERLAIN, J.   *Queen Elizabeth's progresses* (1821).

CHERRY, Bridget and PEVSNER, Nikolaus   Buildings of England: *London 3; north-west* (1991).

COLLINS, Desmond   *Early man in West Middlesex* (HMSO 1978).

COTTON, MILLS and CLEGG   *Archaeology of West Middlesex* (Hillingdon Borough Libraries 1986).

DAWICK, J.   *The provision of education in Uxbridge in the nineteenth century* (ms. 1980).

FAULKNER, Alan   *Grand Junction Canal* (1972).

FOXE, John   *Book of Martyrs* (1554).

GOODE, C.T.   *Railways of Uxbridge* (1983).

GOVER, J., MAWER, A. and STENTON, F.M.   *Place Names of Middlesex* (1942).

GRIFFITHS, D.M.   *200 not out: a history of Uxbridge Cricket Club* (1989).

HEARMON, C.   *Uxbridge: a concise history* (Hillingdon Borough Liberaries, 2nd ed. 1983).

HUTSON, Giles   *Recollections of Uxbridge* (Uxbridge Local History and Archives Society 1985).

JARVIS, L.D.   *Free church history of Uxbridge* (1953).

LYSONS, Daniel   *An historical account of those parishes in the county of Middlesex which are not described in the Environs of London* (1800).

Middlesex and Buckinghamshire Advertiser and Gazette 1854-1994.

MIDDLESEX COUNTY RECORD SOCIETY, ed. JEAFFRESON, J.C.   *Middlesex County Records.* Old Series, 1549-1688 (1887).

PEARCE, K.R.   *Old Meeting Congregational Church, Uxbridge, 1662-1962* (1962).

PEARCE, K.R.   *Short history of the town of Uxbridge* (1970).

REDFORD, G. and RICHES, T.H.   *History of the ancient town and borough of Uxbridge* (1818, reprinted 1887)

STONHAM, C. and FREEMAN, B.   *Historical records of the Middlesex Yeomanry, 1797-1927* (1930).

STRUTT, Thomas   *Peregrinations of a kiddy* (ms. c1873).

TIDY, S.   *A century of public health reform in Uxbridge, 1800-1894* (ms. 1973).

TROTT, Celia   *Story of the Uxbridge Quakers from 1658* (1970).

UXBRIDGE BOROUGH COUNCIL   *Town centre redevelopment* (1963).

UXBRIDGE LOCAL HISTORY AND ARCH-IVES SOCIETY   *Uxbridge Record*, 1964-94.

Victoria History of the County of Middlesex, vols 1-6 (1911-1980).

WEARE, F.W.   *The changing social and economic geography of the lower Colne Valley, 1781-1911* (ms. 1977).

Introduction

For a town which did not exist at the time of the Domesday Survey in 1086 Uxbridge rapidly assumed an importance out of proportion to its size. Originating as a hamlet of the village of Hillingdon, of which parish it remained a chapelry until the nineteenth century, it soon became the most important market centre in West Middlesex. The reasons behind that growth and the subsequent decline are examined here. In recent years Uxbridge has become the administrative and shopping centre of the London Borough of Hillingdon, a factor which has greatly affected the present day appearance of the town.

This book aims to tell, primarily in pictures, the story of Uxbridge from the first traces left by man until the present day. It is based very substantially on *Uxbridge; a concise history*, first published by Hillingdon Borough Libraries in 1983. It has, however, been thoroughly revised and brought up to date with the results of new research. Those who already know the previous book will find much that is new, presented in a different way with the added bonus of many illustrations. We are lucky that there is such a rich visual history for this town, which will serve to remind older residents of what has been lost and to explain to newcomers how Uxbridge comes to be as it is.

The Beginnings

PART OF A MANOR

At the end of the last Ice Age the basis of the present landscape in the Uxbridge area was laid down and the geology and river systems have, apart from minor alterations in the courses and levels of the rivers, remained virtually unchanged. At the beginning of the Mesolithic, or Middle Stone Age, the climate was rather cool and damp; the Colne Valley then was a complex of marsh and fen, interconnecting streams and islands of firmer ground. Recent excavations by the Museum of London of a site near the Treaty House have produced evidence of flint working by mesolithic hunters, the bones of horse, reindeer and red deer and the remains of campfires; charcoal deposits also suggest the use of fire as a means of clearing the surrounding woodland on the valley sides of oak, elm and hazel some time after the site was last used. Archaeological evidence of field boundary ditches suggests a settlement nearby in the Later Bronze Age, although the settlement itself is yet to be found. Recent excavations have revealed some Roman burials, the first evidence that they lived here.

There are isolated examples of human occupation in the following centuries, but not enough to show how or where the people lived. Even the Saxons left little more than their place-names. The name Uxbridge is presumed to mean 'bridge of the Wixan' – the Wixan were a small tribe featured in a number of place-names in north-west Middlesex (Uxendon, Waxlow etc.).

The manors of Colham and Hillingdon are mentioned in the Domesday Book of 1086, but Uxbridge, part of Colham, is not. These two manors covered most of Hillingdon parish. Colham, twice as large as Hillingdon manor, included lands along the Colne, since two and a half water mills are listed as belonging to it (we do not know who owned the other half mill, as it is not listed among the possessions of any of the neighbouring manors). Hillingdon manor had no mills, but a weir, probably on the River Pinn, supplied the villagers with fish. Colham manor was also much better endowed with meadow land: it had enough to

2. *Medieval ploughing*

1. *Uxbridge, 10,000 years ago.*

3. *St John's church, Hillingdon, 1807.*

support twenty-four oxen, that is three plough teams, whereas Hillingdon had only enough to feed half a plough team. And although Hillingdon had as many ploughs in use as the land would support, Colham had six ploughs, though the land could have taken seven, indicating that some useful land was uncultivated. On the other hand, Hillingdon had more woodland and could therefore support more pigs. Finally there was a small vineyard in Colham manor. It has been said that Vine Street in Uxbridge was the site of this vineyard but, alas for the legend, the street was known as Blind Lane until the middle of the nineteenth century.

Much less is known of the people who lived in the two manors. They were not listed by name, only by their status. The most important below the Lord of the Manor were the villagers or villeins, ten of whom lived in Colham and two in Hillingdon. Below them were the smallholders or bordars of whom, again, ten lived in Colham and two in Hillingdon. The lowest in status of the freemen were the cottagers, four in Colham and two in Hillingdon, and also working on the Colham estate were eight slaves. Hillingdon also

had two resident Frenchmen, probably Normans, with their own workers. Altogether forty-two men were listed, which indicates a population of around 200 in the whole area. There was a church to serve these people, as a priest is listed for Colham, although the church is assumed to be that which became St John the Baptist at Hillingdon.

Both Colham and Hillingdon manors had been owned by men who probably spent most of their time at the court of King Edward the Confessor. Wigot of Wallingford, a close kinsman of the king, not only held Colham, but had land in eleven counties; Ulf, one of Edward's military retainers, held Hillingdon. After the Conquest, these men were replaced by Roger de Montgomery, Earl of Shrewsbury, a cousin of William the Conqueror, whose estates in Middlesex on the western boundary of the county were grouped into the Honor of Wallingford. In 1107 this Honor included 'Coleham-cum-Woxbrigge' – a clear reference to Uxbridge. A hundred years after the Domesday Book, in about 1189, the then owner of the Honor proclaimed in a document: 'Gilbert Basset to all Barons of the Honor of Wallingford, and his neighbours

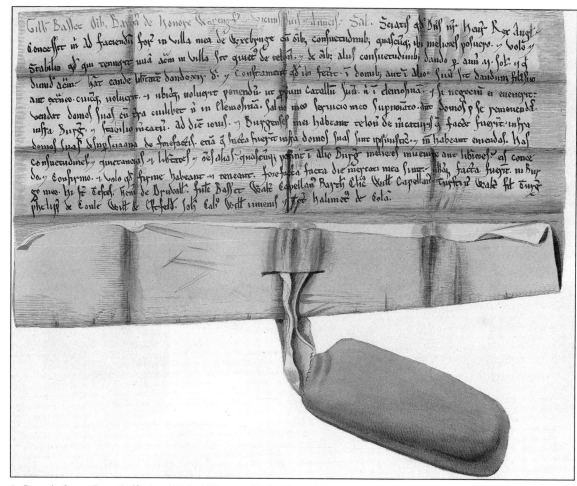

4. *Basset's Grant. From Redford and Riches'* History of Uxbridge, *1818.*

and friends, greeting. Know ye that our Lord Henry, King of England, hath granted to me liberty to make a market in my town of Wxebruge'. The market was to be held each Thursday and all profits arising from it were to belong to Basset; any man who held at least half an acre within the town was exempt from tolls on payment of an annual fine. By 1239 the town also had a fair held each St Margaret's Day and in 1294 the right to hold a second annual fair at Michaelmas, and a Monday market, was granted to the lord of Colham.

A MARKET ATTRACTION

Not only was the market an attraction in itself, but Uxbridge was ideally situated on a main road at a river crossing. Farmers and merchants came from all over Middlesex and Buckinghamshire and gradually Uxbridge expanded, its houses straggling either side of the main street, with a few following the line of a

5. *St Margaret's chapel, Uxbridge, by Daniel King, to illustrate Camden's* Britannia, *1610.*

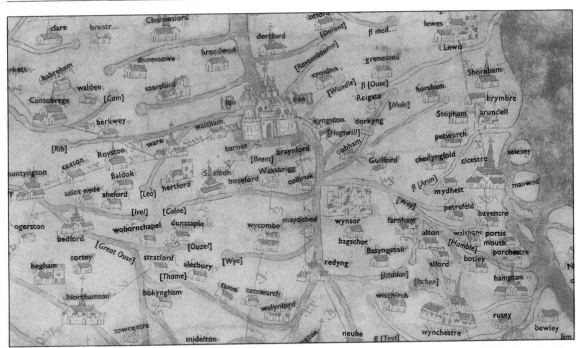

6. *Gough map, c1360. This map is orientated east-west rather than north-south. Uxbridge, spelt 'Waxsbrigg' is in the centre of this extract, just below London which is denoted by a castle. The rivers Thames and Brent are depicted out of proportion. Other local places shown are Brentford, Colnbrook and Windsor.*

7. *The font, St Margaret's. From Redford and Riches' History of Uxbridge.*

side road to Windsor. As the population grew, the mother church at Hillingdon could not cope and about 1200 a chapel-of-ease, dedicated to St Margaret, was built in Uxbridge at the junction of the main street and the road to Windsor, presumably in the market place. Although all the church services could be held there, it did not have a burial ground; in a document of 1200 Radulf, the chaplain of Uxbridge is listed as a witness, the first mention of a priest here.

This rapid increase in population and importance is reflected in the fact that Uxbridge was one of only two Middlesex townships (the other was Brentford) to be represented at the first Parliament of Edward I in 1275. Furthermore, from 1293 and possibly earlier, all the manorial courts of the manors that formed the Honor of Wallingford, were held here – this pertained until the 19th century, when manor courts were abolished. In about 1335 a Muster of men needed for military service required Colham manor to supply 57 footmen and Uxbridge 61, a clear indication of Uxbridge's importance within the manor of which it was once just a small village. The road from London to Oxford and beyond was one of the major routes of medieval England and is one of the five main roads out of London on what is known as the Gough map of about 1360 and we know that in 1314 the men employed to take horses to Oxford for the transportation of the body of Piers Gaveston to Kings Langley spent a night in Uxbridge. Despite what would have been heavy traffic for the period, with farmers coming to market and people travelling longer distances, the road surface was poor so that in wet weather it became a quagmire, and as early as 1358 Ellis Waleys of Uxbridge and two men from Acton were granted the right to pave sections of the road in Uxbridge, Acton and places in between.

Part of the importance of Uxbridge was as a crossing point on the River Colne. Presumably a bridge was there by 1107, when it was already part of the place name itself, but the actual structure is only first mentioned in 1377, when a man named Gomme was ordered, as the owner of the ground on which the bridge stood, to repair it as it was in a ruinous condition. According to Redford and Riches' *History of Uxbridge* the bridge at this time was only suitable for foot and horse passengers; wheeled traffic had to use the adjacent ford. The bridge was in two parts, divided by an island in the centre of the river.

The river provided the power for the mills which were another basis for the economic prosperity of Uxbridge. The two mills mentioned in Domesday Book are impossible to identify as throughout the Middle Ages the mills kept changing their names. However, it is safe to say that throughout this period the number of mills along the Colne and the Frays increased – the Frays is probably an artificial waterway constructed at this time to provide power for additional mills. As late as 1419 the Colne was still navigable by small boats, and at least one mill had its own wharf on the river.

THE LOCAL GUILD

Uxbridge, at first dependent on its market for its prosperity, began to develop other trading and manufacturing interests in line with other medieval towns. Until recent times the most important industries in Uxbridge have been flour milling and brewing. There was not, however, a specific trade guild in Uxbridge (one in which membership is restricted to those following a particular craft) as the population was not large enough to support such a specialisation. But there was a guild in Uxbridge, that of St Mary and St Margaret, founded in 1448, which, like many medieval guilds, was a religious organisation for the social and spiritual benefit of members, protecting their welfare while they were alive and praying for their souls after death. It was also wealthy enough to rebuild the south aisle of St Margaret's so that it was large enough to act as the guild's own chapel, for which it provided a chaplain and two chapelwardens. In 1548 the guild owned the George Inn, shops and houses in Uxbridge and land in Cowley Field, together worth £11.

The guild was not the only benefactor of St Margaret's chapel. In 1446, Walter Shiryngton, Chan-

8. *View at the western end of Uxbridge, from Redford and Riches'* History of Uxbridge, *1818; showing the bridge and ford over the Colne and the (then) newly-constructed canal bridge.*

9. *St Margaret's Chapel, 1809, showing the rebuilt south aisle.*

10. *A medieval building in the High Street, demolished in the 1930s. Pen and ink drawing by Clive Rouse, 1927.*

cellor of the Duchy of Lancaster, applied for permission to found a chantry chapel, in which a priest was employed perpetually to say prayers for its benefactor; his chapel was built at the eastern end of the north aisle after 1459, the year of his death and the first priest was named Christopher Thole. Lands in Uxbridge, including the Bull and Cross Keys inns, were bequeathed to supply the income for the upkeep of the chapel.

Both the guild and chantry chapels were dissolved in 1547 and their assets disposed of.

NEW BUILDINGS

We have no idea of what Uxbridge looked like before the end of the fifteenth century as, apart from the church, there are no buildings surviving from that time. We can assume, however, that the buildings were constructed of timber and that the plots were long and narrow, so that as many as possible could front the High Street. The outline of many of them had a reverse S-shape, a characteristic feature often found in planned medieval towns built over former open fields. Then Uxbridge would have comprised little more than the High Street and the Lynch, behind which lay gardens and fields. Towards the end of the fifteenth century the more prosperous tradesmen and innkeepers began to include brick in their buildings, using the substantial deposits of brickearth around Cowley. One of the most important of these new

11. The Treaty House and Lodge, 1812.

12. The Old Tan Yard. Watercolour by Paul Heron, 1892.

houses was that now known as the Crown and Treaty Inn, built in the first half of the sixteenth century as Place House, later the residence of Sir John Bennet. It was then much larger, as the part that remains today is only one third of the original building, and the main road did not then pass as close as it does today, but curved around the gardens to rejoin its present course at the High Bridge.

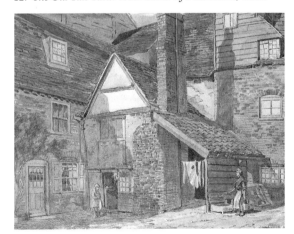

Tudor Uxbridge

PROSPERITY AND CONFLICT

John Leland, the King's Antiquary, visited Uxbridge in the 1540s while on the travels which were to result in the publication of his famous *Itinerary*. His description of Uxbridge is as follows: 'The whole town lieth from the west, rising a little to the south-east. In it is but one long street: but that for timber is well builded. There is a celebrate market once a week, and a great fair once a year at the feast of St. Michael. There is a chapel of ease in the town. The parish church is almost a mile out of town, in the very highway to London, (called Great Hillingdon which is) a token that Uxbridge itself is no very old town.

'There be two wood bridges at the west end of Uxbridge town, and the westernest goeth the main arm of the Colne river. The lesser arm of the Colne goeth under the other [bridge] and each of them serves there a great mill'.

The prosperity of Uxbridge may be gauged from the Subsidy Rolls of the period. During the middle years of his reign Henry VIII was very short of cash, and between 1523 and 1527 levied an annual subsidy on those of his subjects worth more than one pound a year in either goods or wages. From these Rolls we may see the prosperity of Uxbridge relative to the surrounding towns. Of the 153 people taxed in Hillingdon parish seventy-seven were from Uxbridge, and of these the richest 5.2% owned over 34% of the wealth, whereas 31% of the taxpayers owned only 5.6%. These statistics include, of course, only those rich enough to be taxed; for there were many others too poor to pay any taxes at all. In other, similar, towns about a third of the population escaped tax. If this were true of Uxbridge it would make the total population of the town somewhere around 600, but this is only a very rough estimate.

Prosperity brought municipal conflict. Since Gilbert Basset had been granted his charter in 1187 the town had been run as part of the manor of Colham, and in turn as part of the Honor of Wallingford. But growing Uxbridge began to resent this outside control. Matters deteriorated in the early sixteenth century, when one of the Uxbridge constables was attacked and killed by the bailiff of Colham manor and his men, but pressing grievances were not resolved until 1630 and the town was still governed by the Honor Court until its abolition in 1813.

UXBRIDGE MARTYRS

In the bitter religious controversies of the 16th century, Uxbridge was not left untouched. In 1521 a number of Uxbridge men and women were punished

13. *The execution of John Denley. From Foxe's* Book of Martyrs.

for Protestant heresy, and among the religious houses suppressed by Henry VIII, compiled by Leland, was the monastery of St Mary at Uxbridge, founded by Hugh Rowse. However, this is the only reference to such a monastery and it may be that Leland was confusing it with the guild of St Mary and St Margaret already noted. In the Marian persecution after the death of Edward VI three Protestants were burnt at the stake in Uxbridge. They were not local men, but their punishment was intended to set an example to the local people. The three included Robert Smith, a cleric from Windsor, and John Denley, a gentleman of Kent, who went to the stake after torture on the orders of Bonner, Bishop of London. In Foxe's *Book of Martyrs* there is a vivid description of the death of Denley: 'Being set in the fire with the burning flame about him, he sung in it a Psalm. Then cruel Doctor Story

14. *Gateway to the Burial Ground. W.E. Edwards, 1904.*

being there present, commanded one of the tormentors to hurl a Faggot at him, whereupon being hurt therewith upon the face that he bled again, he left his singing, and clapt both his hands on his face. Truly, quoth Dr. Story, to him that hurled the Faggot, thou hast mar'd a good old Song.' The third man to die was Patrick Packingham, an itinerant workman, who was executed on the 28 August the same year. The burnings took place on Lynch Green, close to the site of the old burial ground, where there is now a memorial to the martyrs.

DEPENDENCE ON CORN

The increased trade in Uxbridge in the 16th century is demonstrated by two things. First, the market house, built only at the beginning of the century, was rebuilt larger in 1561, this time at the eastern end of the present building. It was nearly square, being forty by forty-five feet and took up nearly half the width of the High Street, leaving only twenty-one feet of roadway, while the entrance to the Lynch was reduced to only eight feet. Though we have these details we have no picture of this building. Secondly, the number of inns in Uxbridge to cope with travellers was marked. William Camden in the 1580s described Uxbridge as 'full of inns.'

Prosperity in Uxbridge, however, was not consistent. Dependence on corn by both the market and the milling industry made the town vulnerable to fluctuations in the harvest, and when that failed, as it did in the years 1586-7, the town was in 'great distresse for want of corn'. Furthermore, the Justices of the Peace for Hertfordshire and Buckinghamshire forbade the carrying of any corn to Uxbridge because of the scarcity in their own areas. They were requested by the Privy Council to allow farmers who normally took corn to Uxbridge to carry a proportion of their usual load to relieve the dearth in the town. This reliance on corn of Uxbridge's economy was to have serious repercussions later in its history.

LOCAL CHARITIES

This populous town was, however, still only a chapelry of Hillingdon, without its own burial ground and as the population increased this was clearly inconvenient. Therefore, in 1576 the Earl of Derby, then lord of the manor, gave a piece of land adjoining Lynch Green for use as a burial ground, and it was enclosed by a wall at the expense of Margery Legie, a widow: there is an inscription over the gateway to the ground

commemorating this. For every person buried in the new ground the inhabitants of Uxbridge had to pay the church at Hillingdon two pence, as the revenue from burials was a valuable part of church income.

The mid-sixteenth century in Uxbridge saw a large number of charities established. This implies two things: that there were people rich enough to endow them and a large number of poor people to benefit. The oldest charity was that set up by William Skydmore, ironmonger of London but native of Uxbridge, in 1500. This provided twelvepence worth of bread for distribution to the poor after divine service each Sunday at St Margaret's. John Marsh's charity of 1557, administered by the Mercers' Company, supplied twenty-four poor people with two shillings worth of bread every Sunday. Robert Wolman left money from his Hillingdon, Cowley and London properties to maintain a school in Uxbridge, but it was never built. John Garrett, brewer of Uxbridge, left the income from various properties in Uxbridge, including shops and stalls in the market, to be paid by the Burgesses of Kingston-upon-Thames to the poor of Uxbridge.

IN THE COURTS

The records of the Middlesex County Courts have many references to Uxbridge people bound over to keep the peace or indicted for theft. Penalties were very severe; for example, in 1571 Lewis Jones of London stole some clothes and other goods from Hugh Nevill of Uxbridge worth nearly twenty-six shillings, and for this was sentenced to be hanged. Fights could also get out of hand. In 1586 five Uxbridge men 'were fighting together in the highway at Woxbridge with swords and staves'; John Bradley tried to stop them but was hit over the head and died instantly. The man who hit him, Robert Ingledon, was indicted for murder, but no sentence is recorded.

The court records also throw light on local amusements. In March 1576 'at Ruyslippe Co. Midd., Arthur Reynolds, husbandman...(etc.)...all of Ruyslippe aforesaid, Thomas Darcye of Woxbridge yoman, and William Davye Taylor, Roger Okeley yoman, Thomas Harker husbandman, William Raynar husbandman, and Richard Parsonne husbandman, all seven of Woxbridge aforesaid, with unknown malefactors to the number of a hundred, assembled themselves unlawfully and played a certain unlawfull game, called footeball, by reason of which unlawfull game there rose amongst them a great affray, likely to result in homicides and serious accidents".

A Time of Turmoil

PLAGUE IN UXBRIDGE

London was consumed by plague in 1603, so severe that the Coronation of James I was postponed. Uxbridge did not escape it. Though thought to have come in on rags used for making paper, it could just as easily have been brought by one of the many travellers from the city. In that year 176 people died of the plague out of the 205 buried in Uxbridge. It was almost certainly a disaster for the trade of the town, its market and its supporting agriculture. The plague returned in 1625, when 136 out of 162 burials were the result of the disease, and again in 1636, when the Middlesex Sessions levied a rate on county parishes to support those stricken with plague in the London area: Uxbridge was assessed at thirty shillings a week and Hillingdon at forty shillings. But in the Great Plague of 1665 Uxbridge escaped fairly lightly; only half the eighty-one deaths that year were caused by plague.

THE TOLL DISPUTE

In July 1602, eight months before she died, Queen Elizabeth I visited the Countess of Derby at Harefield Place, a visit marked by pouring rain. At this time the lordship of the manor of Colham was held by the Countess, the last of the Derby family to do so. She had several children from previous marriages and would hold court at Harefield Place with all her family gathered about her. One of her protégés was the poet Milton, then a young man living at Horton a few miles away – his masque *Arcades* was written for the Countess and first performed at Harefield in 1633.

As one of the perquisites of the manor Lady Derby was entitled, under the terms laid down in Basset's Grant, to the tolls raised at Uxbridge market. It was her custom at the Manor Court, after formal acknowledgement of her right to the tolls, to hand all the money back to the bailiffs to expend on charitable purposes in the town. However, in 1630 certain of the townsfolk, calling themselves burgesses, although they had no legal right to do so, reassessed Basset's Grant. They misread the document and thought that it said that they, rather than the Lord of the Manor, were entitled to the profits of the market. At the Court Leet at Easter that year the bailiffs and 'burgesses' refused to acknowledge the Countess's right to the

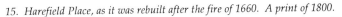

15. *Harefield Place, as it was rebuilt after the fire of 1660. A print of 1800.*

16. Lady Derby's tomb in Harefield Church.

17. John Milton

tolls and after discussion her steward postponed the meeting until Whitsun, but when he returned for that meeting he found the Court Room, over the Market House, locked against him. Although he tried to hold the meeting nearby no decision could be obtained and the matter was adjourned again until July, but there was still no settlement. The Countess by now was justifiably annoyed. On 18 April 1631 she sent an order to the bailiffs in which she said that although hitherto she had allowed them to collect and distribute the tolls, from henceforth she would arrange for their collection and distribution as she saw fit.

After the receipt of this order matters simmered for a few months, until July. At the Fair of St Margaret on 20 July, the Countess's steward arrived to collect the tolls from the cattle market. The toll was one penny each from the buyer and seller of an animal, but the rebellious users of the Market, based on their interpretation of Basset's charter, thought that the Countess was entitled to only a penny a beast – this in itself an admission that she was entitled to a toll. The dispute continued and on a following day, when the Countess's two stewards began to collect the toll-

corn, an armed mob of about forty, led by a man called Baker, descended on them, tore their clothes and threw them out of the market. At this point William Jarman, a constable, arrived. It was his duty to stop the unlawful assembly and he stood in the market place calling out 'Oyez! Oyez! Let no-one presume to enter the Market House at his peril!' No-one took any notice, and when Baker told Jarman to arrest one of the Countess's stewards he did not know what to do. Then Sir Edward Carr, Justice of the Peace, arrived. He too tried to calm the situation, but Baker, who would have none of it even posted his own man on the stairs up to the room over the Market House where the toll-corn was stored, armed with a drawn sword, a gun and a pistol loaded with hail shot.

Trouble broke out again on the market day of the following week. As the Countess's servant, Richard Lee, an elderly gentleman, was taking the toll-corn from the cart of a Mrs Jeffreys he was attacked by Baker and several others, all armed. He was pulled out of his cart, almost losing his boot in the process, and severely bruised. Several hundred inhabitants then rioted and appropriated the toll-corn for themselves.

The Countess of Derby immediately started legal proceedings and writs were issued by the Crown. In Court the Uxbridge 'burgesses' pleaded that they were only claiming their rights as laid down in Basset's Grant. The document was produced but neither the judge nor the burgesses' council could read the Latin. However, Mr Moy, acting for the Countess, could do so and he proved her right to the tolls. The Court decided in her favour, but still the rioting

18. Mural by Barbara Jones depicting the events of 1630-33.

continued, so that the Countess commenced a suit in the Court of Star Chamber, which effectively frightened her opponents into submission. Twenty of them, with Edmund Baker at their head, humbly petitioned the Countess to stop the Star Chamber proceedings; they offered to submit entirely to her goodwill and not dispute the tolls. However, once the case had come to Star Chamber it could not be stopped; the result was that Baker and the other burgesses were fined £220 – £20 for the King and £200 for Lady Derby, which she agreed not to impose on their further apology. The whole affair ended amicably with a feast held at the Court Leet on 1 October 1633 and a gift of venison from Lady Derby. (A mural, shown above, by Barbara Jones depicting scenes from these events can be seen in the Central Library, Uxbridge.)

INTERLUDES IN THE CIVIL WARS

The events leading up to the Civil Wars of the 17th century are outside the scope of this book. Suffice it to say that when Charles I called what was later known as the Long Parliament in October 1640, he was assembling his enemies together. He needed money, which only they could provide; but Parliament would not agree unless the King acceded to their demands. In 1641 Parliament drew up a manifesto, known as the Protestation, in which each Member swore to uphold the King, Parliament, the rights of individuals and the Protestant religion as expressed in the Church of England. Although this purported to be in defence of King, Church and Constitution, it was in effect an attack on Charles and his friends. When the King left London in January 1642 the obligation to sign the oath was extended to all males over the age of eighteen. A total of 288 Uxbridge men signed it in the church on

19. *The Crown Inn, from the* Uxbridge Panorama, *c1800.*

23 February 1642, in the presence of Thomas Twist, minister of St Margaret's, the churchwardens and constables – none is listed as having refused. This is the first indication we have had for some time of the size of the population of Uxbridge, which may therefore be estimated at around 1,000 at this date. Although by modern standards this is not large, in the seventeenth century Uxbridge was regarded as a fairly populous small town. The population of the rest of the parish of Hillingdon was somewhere around 800, with 233 men signing the Protestation oath.

By the end of 1644 Charles I appeared to be losing the Civil War. He had lost the greater part of his soldiers and the whole of the north of England after the Battle of Marston Moor in July of that year; Cromwell was in the process of reorganising the New Model Army and in January 1645 Archbishop Laud of Canterbury, one of the King's principal supporters, was executed. Negotiations for a peace treaty began immediately after Marston Moor, the initiative coming from Charles. Parliament decided to hold the discussions in the town of Uxbridge, which supported their cause, it being conveniently between the Royal headquarters in Oxford and the Parliamentary stronghold of London. The proposed Treaty was an attempt by the Presbyterian party and the Scots to achieve their own ends; Cromwell and his Independents took no part. Thirty-two Commissioners were appointed; sixteen for each side. Including all their assistants, servants and soldiers and all the people who must have flocked to Uxbridge to see the great events, the town must have been very full indeed for those few weeks in January and February 1645.

20. *The rear of the George Inn.*

Edward Hyde, Earl of Clarendon, one of the King's Commissioners, has left a full description of those weeks in his *History of the Great Rebellion and Civil Wars*, which Redford and Riches quote at length. The King's Commissioners were given the whole of the south side of the High Street, with the exception of one house, for their accommodation and they took the Crown Inn for their headquarters. The Parliament men had the north side, with the George as their base. The atmosphere on each side of the street seems to have been markedly different, even allowing for Clarendon's bias. The King's men spent their time seeing friends and behaving as though they were in their own homes, but among the Roundheads there was an atmosphere of gloom and mistrust.

The actual negotiations took place in the building now known as the Crown and Treaty House Inn.

21. *Edward Hyde, Earl of Clarendon, one of the Parliamentary Commissioners.*

Clarendon says: 'There was a good House at the end of the Town, which was provided for the Treaty, where there was a fair room in the middle of the House, handsomely dressed up for the Commissioners to sit in; a large square table being placed in the middle with Seats for the Commissioners, one side being sufficient for those of either party; and a Rail for others who should be thought necessary to be present, which went round. There were many other Rooms on either side of this Great Room, for the Commissioners on either side to retire to, when they thought fit to consult by themselves, and to return again to Publick

22. *The Treaty House, c1810.*

Debate, and there being good Staires at either end of the House, they never went through each others Quarters, nor met but in the Great Room.' A room in the existing building has traditionally been known as that in which the Treaty was discussed. This, however, is unlikely. The actual room was almost certainly in the central wing demolished in the eighteenth century and the room remaining is more probably one of those to which the Commissioners retired. (In 1924 its panelling was sold to an American and installed in his office in the Empire State Building, New York. The panelling was returned to England as a Coronation gift to Queen Elizabeth II in 1953 and restored to the inn, although it still remains the property of the Queen. During the eighteenth century the main block and one side wing were demolished and the remaining building divided into several tenements. In 1785 improvements to the High Street meant that the line of the road was taken straight through the Treaty House gardens. Soon after this the building became an inn, with stabling for over forty horses.)

The day set for the opening of the Treaty negotiations was also a market day. Traditionally a sermon was preached at St Margaret's, and many of the visitors, townsfolk and market traders went to church that day. The sermon was preached by Christopher Love, a staunch Puritan, then chaplain to the garrison

23. *The panelled room in the Treaty House; a print of 1850.*

24. *Christopher Love.*

at Windsor Castle. He told the people not to expect any good from the Treaty, 'for that they come from Oxford with their hearts full of blood, and that there was as great a distance between this Treaty and Peace as between Heaven and Hell'. Love was clearly intending to stir up the people and cause a riot against the King's Commissioners. He was expelled from Uxbridge, but not otherwise punished for these seditious remarks, but his career ended on the scaffold in 1651, when he was executed for High Treason while trying to restore the monarchy!

There was never any real expectation that the peace negotiations would achieve any result and after three weeks the Commissioners separated and returned to their respective headquarters. Uxbridge settled back once more into its usual way of life.

The town had been garrisoned by Parliamentary troops since hostilities began in 1642. They cannot have been very alert, for in April 1646 Charles I escaped from Oxford and passed through Uxbridge to stop at the Red Lion inn, Hillingdon, where for several hours he refreshed himself before continuing his journey. In June 1647, the Parliamentary Army, under the command of Oliver Cromwell, made its headquarters in Uxbridge as the centre of a line stretching from Staines to Watford. Cromwell himself stayed at the Crown, the former Cavalier headquarters.

25. *The Red Lion, Hillingdon; postcard of c1900.*

26. *Oliver Cromwell.*

THE TOLLS BATTLE RENEWED

The Civil Wars allowed the residents of Uxbridge to have the market tolls wrested from the Lord of the Manor. This was because the new Lord was the Countess of Derby's grandson, Lord Chandos, a Royalist who had left England in 1652. After the Restoration Lord Chandos' successor filed a bill for restitution of the tolls but the result of this action is unknown, and he tried again in 1672, when the verdict was against the town. In 1669 Uxbridge was separated from the manor of Colham and in 1695 the lordship of the new manor of Uxbridge, including its tolls, was sold to seven Uxbridge inhabitants for the sum of £550. Thus the long-running dispute over the market tolls was finally settled. One of the inhabitants of Uxbridge who bought the manor was an Edmund Baker, grandson of the man who fought the Countess of Derby.

THE HEARTH TAX

After the Restoration of 1660 Charles II was perpetually short of money. The Civil Wars had been very expensive, both in money and men. One solution to this problem was the Hearth Tax, imposed from 1662 until 1689, basically a tax of two shillings a year on each domestic hearth. Exemptions were made for those too poor to pay. In 1664 there were, in Uxbridge, 232 occupied houses eligible to pay tax compared with only 179 in the rest of Hillingdon, of which nearly three-quarters were houses with between one and four fireplaces. There were few larger houses, although there were three with twenty hearths. One of these was certainly the Treaty House, the other two were inns. Analysis of these Hearth Tax returns compared with other towns shows that Uxbridge was among the more prosperous of the small market towns.

In fact, Uxbridge expanded towards the end of the century, along the line of the High Street into Hillingdon parish. This was known as Hillingdon End, and although in spirit it was part of Uxbridge it was administratively part of Hillingdon. On the edge of town, sizeable houses, such as Belmont near Uxbridge Common, were erected.

RELIGIOUS TROUBLES

Religious toleration did not improve after the execution of the King in 1649, nor after 1660 when his son was restored to the throne. Under the Commonwealth only Puritans were permitted and Anglicans, Roman Catholics and Quakers were all forbidden to worship. In Uxbridge, the Anglican minister of St Margaret's was replaced by a Puritan and some of the twenty inns in the town were closed. The troubled times worried one man so much that he hid his savings in a wall at Fountains Mill: the coins were not discovered until 1895.

The introduction of the set of Acts after the Restoration known as the Clarendon Code, which enforced worship in the Church of England, affected the town directly. In 1662, Thomas Godboult, the Puritan minister of St. Margaret's, was ejected from his living for refusing to conform to the Code. By this time there were at least two non-conformist sects worshipping in Uxbridge. The Society of Friends, or Quakers, had met in the town since 1658 and formed a small but very influential body in the commercial life of Uxbridge. An early member was William Winch, landlord of the George Inn, and one of the leaders in the dispute with the Countess of Derby: the land on which the present Meeting House stands, then at the rear of the George, was acquired from him in 1676. The first building was erected in 1692; rebuilt in 1817, it is still in use. Also founded in the late seventeenth century was the Old Meeting Congregational Church. In 1662 several ejected Puritan ministers gathered in Uxbridge, the most important of whom was Hezekiah Woodward, ex-vicar of Bray and a former chaplain to Oliver Cromwell. Until his death in 1675 he led, in secret, a body of Strict Independents (later known as Congregationalists) who met in private houses. Their Meeting House was built in 1716 and still stands.

During the seventeenth century, apart from a short time during the Commonwealth, the chapel of St. Margaret's did not have a permanent minister; rather it was administered by the Vicar of Hillingdon, who

27. The Quaker Meeting House, from Redford and Riches' History of Uxbridge, *1818.*

28. The Old Meeting House, from Redford and Riches' History of Uxbridge, *1818.*

performed Divine Service at Uxbridge once a month, and that only in the morning. As the townspeople of Uxbridge had achieved their independence in so many ways this remaining item of outside control was annoying. 'Townsend's Gift' gave Uxbridge some measure of ecclesiastical independence. Under the 1682 will of George Townsend, provision was made for profits from properties in London to support a minister at the chapelries of Uxbridge and Colnbrook. Scholarships were also to be provided for students to attend Pembroke College, Oxford and whenever a vacancy occurred at either Uxbridge or Colnbrook it was to be filled by one of these scholars. The minister

was known as a Lecturer and his duties were to read prayers and preach on Sunday morning and prayers only in the afternoon; all other religious services were still performed by the Vicar of Hillingdon.

Several new charities were established in the seventeenth century. One which had an unusual beginning was founed by Lord Ossulston. Driving through Uxbridge one day in the late 1680s, he ran over and killed a small boy. In reparation he set up a trust to apprentice poor children to handicraft trades. This was one of the more influential and useful charities operating in the town in the eighteenth and nineteenth centuries.

Problems and Improvements

29. *A piece of wooden water pipe.*

A WATER SUPPLY

By the end of the eighteenth century Uxbridge, still dependent for its prosperity on markets, mills and inns, was the most considerable market town in Middlesex and the increased wealth brought by trade gradually resulted in improvements in the town's amenities.

The first to benefit a large number of the inhabitants came in 1701. Mr John Yarnold constructed a water-works to supply water, in wooden pipes, from the Colne to Uxbridge. For a pound a year the water was laid on to individual houses; it was supplied to the top of the town in the morning and the bottom in the afternoon one day and vice-versa the next. The water-works were badly damaged during the digging of the Grand Junction Canal and the supply ceased in 1799 and after this the town was without a regular supply of clean water until wells were dug in 1800.

THE POOR IN THEIR MIDST

Money for poor relief came from rates levied on householders, administered by two Overseers of the Poor elected annually. As they were themselves house-holders they had a vested interest in keeping the rates as low as possible.

The system of providing for the 'deserving' poor was in two parts, usually called 'Indoor' and 'Out-door' relief. Those too old, too young or too sick to take care of themselves were taken into the work-house, built in 1728 on Lynch Green. It was not a pleasant place. A correspondent to the *Uxbridge Note Book* wrote: 'Being brought the Workhouse was, in days past, an evil too dreadful to be contemplated. The possibility of such an event drove the sluggard from his bed, the drunkard from his pot and the sensualist from his low pleasures. To keep an aged parent from the parish was the pride and glory of children, and the dread of parochial relief to the child, embittered the passing moments of the dying parent.' Throughout the eighteenth century the management of the workhouse was contracted out; that is, some-one agreed, for a fixed sum each year, to manage it. No records survive to show how the workhouse was run, but the system was harsh and open to corruption. Most contractors endeavoured to make as much profit for themselves while spending as little as possible on the paupers in their charge. In 1775 there were sixty inmates, and the poor rate yielded £410. This was augmented by charities and also by the Lords in Trust

(see below), who spent an increasing amount of the manorial profits on poor relief. In 1748 they spent £58 on occasional relief to ninety-five townspeople, twelve non-townspeople and sixteen tenants of the almshouses, and by 1778 almost two-thirds of the manorial profits of £378 were spent in this way.

EDUCATING THE POOR

Although the Lecturer of St Margaret's chapel had a reasonable income under the terms of George Townsend's will (see page 28), he did not have a permanent residence in the town. In 1705, therefore, the people of Uxbridge subscribed £126, with another £200 borrowed, to build him a house. This was erected in an acre of land in Cowley Field behind Vine Street, with the condition that the Lecturer taught six poor boys reading and writing in rooms at the workhouse. Girls were educated in the Lynch. A room over the Market House was also used as a schoolroom, prob-ably for the boys. From the early eighteenth century part of the profits from the market were used to educate twenty boys and twenty-one girls.

This development was made possible by a change in the government of the town. In 1729 the surviving representatives of the five men who had bought the manor of Uxbridge in 1695 conveyed their responsi-bilities to seven trustees, thereafter known as the Lords of the Manor in Trust, who were to use mano-rial profits for charitable purposes. The final Manor Court Leet, before it was abolished by the Lords in Trust, was held in 1727. This was an important meet-ing for, amongst other things, it led to a survey of the manor in which the boundaries of Uxbridge were defined for the first time. The boundary enclosed an area of eighty-five acres. The westernmost point was the High Bridge over the Colne, with Vine Street (then known as Blind or Woolwind Lane) forming the eastern boundary. The River Frays was on the south, while the northern boundary, difficult to define be-cause it ran across fields, followed roughly the line of the modern York Road.

30. *The White Horse Inn, from the* Uxbridge Panorama. *The inn sign over the entrance porch was a large statue of a white horse.*

RURAL REALITIES

In 1828 a correspondent to the *Uxbridge Note Book* felt impelled to correct a falsely Utopian picture of eighteenth-century Uxbridge by giving his own account of the town in the early years of the century. A large part of his letter is worth quoting: 'Two or three facts were related to me by a Magistrate of a neighbouring county who died some years ago at a very advanced age, which, if correct, go far to prove exactly the reverse of some of Juvenal's [the previous correspondent] statements respecting our ancestors. Somewhat more than a century ago (about 1720) the high road through the Town was in so bad a state, and the nuisances and annoyances of all kinds so intolerable, that travellers were accustomed carefully to avoid passing through it, by crossing from Hillingdon to High Bridge over the waste lands on the northeast side of the Town. This speaks volumes against the boasted virtues, industry and absence of misery of our forebears. My informant recollected the Publicans' signs swinging from crossbeams over the street, the middle of which was a deep muddy kennel that received and retained the filth of the town so that its poisonous miasma was plentifully conveyed to the lungs of the inhabitants.

'When Sir John Fielding presided over the police of the metropolis, the number and turpitude of the criminals brought before him from the Lynch induced him to call it Hell. This street was at that time notoriously the haunt of Thieves, Pickpockets etc. who exercised their callings in open day; and no-one thought of encountering the risk of passing through it by night.

'There are still old inhabitants who recollect Hawke and other notorious Highwaymen living there publicly, and, under pretence that they would never rob an Uxbridge man, and giving it out as their determination that they would never be taken alive, they defied the law with impunity.

'Even down to the period when Juvenal tells us "joy and gladness beamed in every countenance" the generality of tradesmen in other points respectable, indulged habitually in gluttony and drunkenness. They sallied forth at midnight, pulled down their neighbours' shutters – broke their windows and even into their houses – painted the 'White Horse' black etc. Their feasting began in the morning – the sole business of their lives appeared to be eating and drinking – and indulging in practical jokes without counting the cost. Woe to Juvenal's Vines and Fig-trees – he never heard of the "Marlow Men"' (The 'Marlow Men' were Uxbridge's own version of the notorious Mohocks of eighteenth-century London.)

THE STORY OF WILLIAM HAWKE

William Hawke, the highwayman mentioned above, was born in Uxbridge about 1750. At a young age he took to a life of crime and was transported to America in 1771, from which he escaped and returned home, to marry. Though arrested again, he escaped once more, this time from Tothill prison, and then resumed his criminal career. On 28 March 1774, when a Captain Cunningham and a Mr Hart were travelling in a coach, soon after passing through Knightsbridge they heard someone shout, "Damn your eyes, stop! Or I'll blow your brains out". A moment later Hawke thrust a pistol through the coach window and demanded Hart's money. Mr Hart, not carrying much cash, handed over 1/6d and then some halfpennies. Hawke was disgusted, "Damn you, d'ye think I'll accept of halfpence?" he said. Meanwhile Captain Cunningham, who had been drinking, tried to hide his pocketbook. When Hawke saw this he pointed the pistol at his head and threatened to shoot if the Captain did not instantly deliver. "Fire away and be damned" responded the Captain, so Hawke did, but the bullet passed between the Captain's shoulder and his coat. Hawke dismounted to search the coach and his second pistol misfired as the Captain, if not both gentlemen, resisted him. As he tried to reload they pelted him with stones picked up from the road and as he searched the coach the Captain beat Hawke's horse with a stick. Despite all this Hawke managed to ride away but he was arrested after his wife was traced following a visit to Uxbridge. He was tried and hanged at Tyburn on 1 July 1774, and was buried at Uxbridge.

31. Hawke robs Captain Cunningham and Mr Hart.

32. William Hawke in Newgate Prison. Both illustrations from the Newgate Calendar.

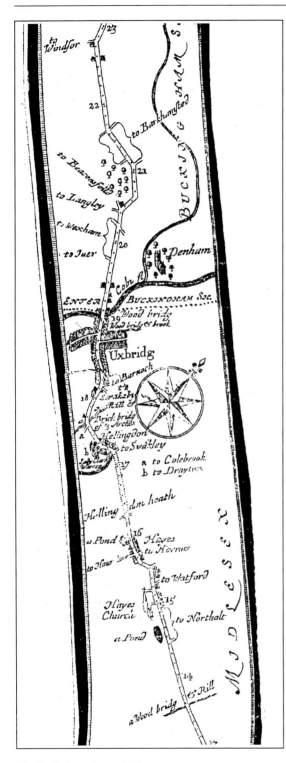

33. Ogilby's road map, 1695.

A Traveller's Rest

A PLACE OF INNS

The food and drink trades were an important part of the economy of Uxbridge. In the eighteenth century, well over a quarter of the population of the town was employed in their supply. Harman's Brewery was founded in about 1729 and continued to brew beer until 1964, and Norton's Brewery began in 1750, on the north side of the High Street. Later in the century the Norton family expanded into other areas of business, particularly banking, and their interest in brewing had ceased by the 1830s. The inns supplied not only food and drink but were also a vital part of nearly all aspects of eighteenth-century life. There were four major inns in Uxbridge; the Crown, the George, the White Horse and the King's Arms. These were posting inns, providing a meal and a change of horses for travellers, as well as overnight accommodation. Fifteen miles was about the furthest distance a team of horses could travel at any speed while pulling a coach and Uxbridge was about that distance on the Oxford Road from Tyburn (now Marble Arch) and from High Wycombe.

IMPROVING THE ROADS

The amount of traffic using the Uxbridge Road was greatly increased when the roads were improved with the introduction of turnpikes. Until this time the responsibility of repairing any road fell on the parish through which it passed. This was particularly hard on those parishes which included a heavily used main road, and consequently repairs were often badly done or not at all. With a Turnpike Act a Board of Trustees took over a length of road, became responsible for its maintenance, and in return could charge tolls for its use. The first Act for repairing and improving the road between Tyburn and Uxbridge was passed in 1714. This Act cost the Trustees £162.11.6d, with expenses ranging from £55 for the fee for the Bill to be passed to the House of Lords, to sixpence to a man to take the Act to the printers. Sixty-nine trustees were named, many of whom were local gentry, such as the Pagets of West Drayton, the Newdigates of Harefield and Sir Robert Vyner of Ickenham, as well as some of the more prosperous local tradesmen. The turnpike gates for Uxbridge were outside each end of the town, where the jurisdiction of two different trusts ended. The Tyburn to Uxbridge Trust gate was near the top of the Greenway, at what is now called Turnpike Lane and the Aylesbury and Wendover Trust Gate was in Denham.

The setting up of a Turnpike Trust did not necessarily result in improvements, as was found in many

34. *Harman's Brewery, shortly before demolition in the 1960s.*

35. *The King's Arms, by W.E. Edwards c1925.*

parts of the country. Writing in 1798 in his *View of the Agriculture of Middlesex*, John Middleton states: 'The road from Tyburn through Uxbridge is supposed to have more broad-wheeled waggons pass over it than any other road in the country. Therefore, if broad wheels were advantageous to the roads, this would be in high condition, as it is certainly sufficiently

rolled; and it has also the advantage of lying on a bed of gravel. But these, and the present management, are insufficient to keep it in repair.

'During the whole of the winter of 1797-8, there was but one passable track on this road, and that was less than six feet wide, and was eight inches deep in fluid mud. All the rest of the road was from a foot to eighteen inches deep in adhesive mud.

'This track was thronged with waggons (many of them drawn by ten horses and having broad wheels, even to sixteen inches wide) and farmers' six inch wheel carts which occupied almost the whole of this confined space. It was therefore with great difficulty, and some danger, that horsemen and light carriages could pass.

'The road continued in this infamous condition during the whole winter half-year. No exertions were made towards cleansing it, although an expenditure of such a trifle as twenty-pounds, in the employment of a road-scraper drawn by one horse, would have effectively kept it clean and dry; and would also have prevented the destruction of upwards of three hundred pounds' worth of materials, that were reduced to mud by being soaked and ground, for six months, in water mixed with pounded flints.

'The only labourers to be seen on the road, during several succeeding months, were those of a neighbouring gentleman; and they were employed in carting the footpath to his enclosures.

'The tolls taken at the gates amount to a very large

36. *Hillingdon Turnpike c1840*

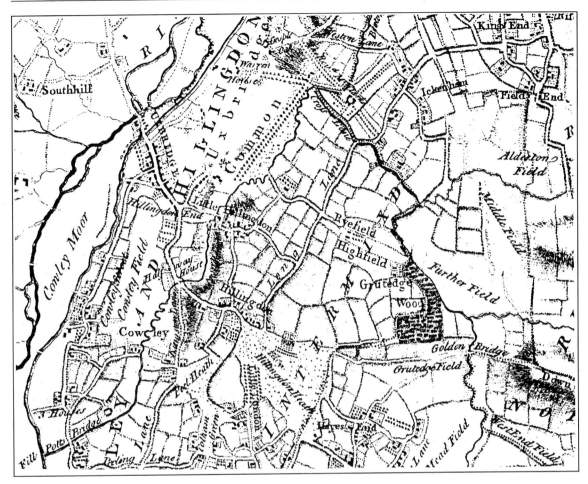

37. *Part of John Rocque's map of Middlesex, 1754.*

sum annually; and as nothing is done towards keeping the road in repair, an enquiry ought to be instituted, as to what becomes of the money so collected.

'I do not mean, in the smallest degree, to insinuate that any of the trustees apply the principal to their own use, but the public have a right to expect that the tolls should be let for the greatest possible sum, and that the money raised should be laid out in such a manner as to render the road clean and comfortable.

Despite Middleton's comments the turnpikes did improve travel between Uxbridge and London and by the 1780s it took just two hours to travel the distance. However, while travel on the open road was improved, delays were still caused in Uxbridge. The old Market House had reduced the width of the High Street to only twenty-one feet – just enough for two carriages to pass, and on market days even this was impossible. At the west end of the High Street the road between the bridge over the River Frays and the High

Bridge was very narrow and circuitous as it passed around the outskirts of the grounds of the Treaty House. The High Bridge was rebuilt in 1768 as a seven-arch brick bridge.

REBUILDING THE MARKET

In 1785 an Act of Parliament was obtained to allow the demolition of the old Market House and the straightening of the road abutting it. At the same time the opportunity was taken to pave and light some of the main footpaths in the town. According to Redford and Riches 'the improvements made in the town....were numerous and very considerable; so much so, as to give it quite a new aspect and make it assume to strangers, the appearance of being built in modern times.'

The new Market House, symbolising the supreme importance to the town of the corn trade, was the most

38. Uxbridge Market House. Watercolour by Edward Hassel, c1790.

39. Plan of intended road improvements at the Treaty House and High Bridge.

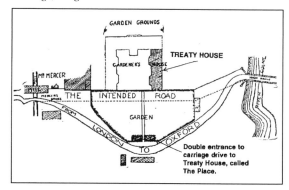

striking building in late 18th-century Uxbridge. The first stone was laid on 28 May 1788 to the accompaniment of church bells, and the building, designed by Thomas Neill and built by Messrs Busby, Best & Powell, was completed within a year at a cost of £3000. It was paid for by voluntary subscription and from a loan which was repaid by increased revenue from tolls. It was owned by the Lords in Trust, and continued to be so until 1981, when it was sold to an insurance company. The imposing neo-classical building filled the whole area between the two entrances to Windsor Street, with a frontage to the High Street. The upper rooms were designed to store corn, but they were soon used for other functions. Both the Boys' Free School and the Girls' School of Industry were housed there, as were such organisations as the Reading Society, the Auxiliary Bible Society and the Savings Bank.

Chapels and Amenities

CHAPELS

Though lacking the fervour of the seventeenth century, non-conformist religious sects in Uxbridge were still active. The Quakers had suffered most from a loss of interest; by 1724 their meetings were poorly attended and the Meeting House so neglected that it had to be rebuilt in 1755. Interest revived, however, towards the end of the century, when the Hulls and other wealthy Quaker families settled in the town. They were rich corn-millers, related to other prominent Quakers, and friends of such people as Elizabeth Fry, who visited them at Uxbridge.

John Wesley, who preached in Hillingdon and Uxbridge in 1754 and 1758, was the inspiration of the evangelical revival that swept through the Church of England in the latter part of the eighteenth century. This movement prompted a group of Anglicans to commence their own meetings in a room at the George Inn in 1770 and by 1796 a meeting house had been erected in the Lynch. It was built in the garden of his house, at his own expense, by Job Arnold Glover, a merchant grocer. This chapel, later known as Provi-

dence Congregational Church, had its own burial ground and soon became one of the most influential forces in Uxbridge, for many of the town's important citizens were members of its congregation. In 1812 the Rev. George Redford was instituted as minister; he was one of the co-authors, in 1818, of the *History of the ancient town and borough of Uxbridge*.

His fellow writer, Thomas Hurry Riches, solicitor and banker, was a member of the still thriving Old Meeting House congregation which, from 1769 until 1789 had as minister the Rev. Dr William Rutherford, an eminent scholar, who opened a school in his house on Uxbridge Common. This was developed by his successor, Rev. Dr Thomas Ebenezer Beasley, and eventually moved to premises in Old Meeting House Yard, later known as Beasley's Yard. This school, known as the Uxbridge School, had a very good

41. *Uxbridge School Token. Awarded to pupils for good work. The tortoise is probably taken from Aesop's fable of the hare and the tortoise.*

40. *Silhouettes of William Hull, his wife and son. Taken on the Chain Pier, Brighton, 1857.*

42. *Watercolour of Providence Chapel, c1800.*

43. *Rev. George Redford, minister of Providence Chapel 1812-27*

reputation and lasted until 1880. At a time when non-conformists were barred from sending their sons to public schools and to Oxford and Cambridge universities, such an establishment was of great value, and quite often provided a better education, since experiments in teaching were more likely to be tried.

Local children, too poor to attend the Uxbridge School, went to a Sunday School set up in the Old Meeting House by 1792.

During the eighteenth century the Church of England was more interested in church fabric than religious disputation. St Margaret's was typical of this period. The first major expenditure was in 1716 when a gallery was built at the west end of the chapel and in 1717 the bells were replaced, a costly and time-consuming business paid for by church rates and donations. The bells were an important part of life; they were rung not only for church services but also whenever there was any important news, and in an age when few people had their own clocks, the church bells acted as an alarm when they rang each morning at five o'clock. The interior of the chapel was not neglected; in 1734 in was 'ceiled and beautified' and further alterations were made in 1771, when an elaborate painted reredos was placed behind the main altar.

44. *Mercer's Mill, from the* Uxbridge Panorama.

45. *Interior of the south aisle of St Margaret's, c1850,*
showing the box pews and the hammer beam roof after it had
been 'ceiled and beautified'.

46. *A plan of the Lynch and Burial Ground, c1790.*

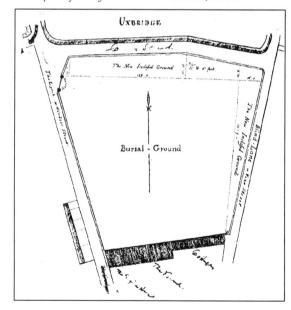

Market and Fairs

THE LARGEST CORN MARKET

At the beginning of the nineteenth century the most important activity in Uxbridge was the Market and the mills connected with it. It was generally known as the largest pitched corn market in the country and the mills supplied London with the bulk of its flour.

Giles Hutson, writing in the 1880s, has described the Market at its peak in the 1830s:

'Early in the morning, even by five or six o'clock, the farmers' waggons laden with corn for sale began to arrive. Many of these waggons came from a considerable distance, from Shepherds Bush, Willesden, Edgware, Hendon in that direction, from Staines, Hounslow, Hampton and other places along the banks of the Thames between Marlow and Kingston, whilst from the district around Rickmansworth many came, and from Chalfont, Wycombe, Amersham and Missenden in Buckinghamshire, and even from the country about Chinnor in Oxfordshire, considerable quantities were brought.

'At eight o'clock the first Market bell was rung, when lenten corn, that is oats, barley and other spring corn sown about the time of Lent, might be offered. It was against the rules of the Market for any corn to be sold before the ringing of this first bell and then only the kinds first named.

'As the morning advanced a larger number of waggons were constantly arriving loaded with wheat and all of it was pitched in the Market place, one sack upon another, if room for it could be found there, when if not it was placed in the gateways or on any other spare piece of ground in the immediate locality.

'The second bell was rung at twelve o'clock giving notice that the sale of wheat might commence. This prohibition of commencing sales before a given time was made to prevent any enterprising speculator, who had got a priority of news which ensured him prices would go up, stealthily buying up the corn before other dealers had arrived on the ground, and as twelve o'clock was the time agreed upon as suitable for commencing to sell wheat, the Millers and Dealers assembled at that hour and then a scene of great business activity ensued, which lasted about two hours, and during this space the greater part of the grain on offer usually changed hands.

'These sales were effected at this date more frequently by the farmer himself selling his corn to the Miller, although in some cases a middleman or salesman undertook to dispose of it and thus relieved the farmer of all the trouble of dealing.

'This practice gradually grew in favour, until very few growers sold their own corn, and this made room for a considerable number of salesmen as the Market

47. *A busy scene at the Market House.*

48. *Rear of the Market House. From* Rambles round Eton and Harrow, *by A. Rimmer, 1898.*

was a very large one, indeed said at that time to be the largest pitched market in England, that is where the corn was brought in bulk for sale.

'The custom of the market authorities was to take one pint from each sack of corn as the toll and the

49. *Copper scoop used for taking the toll corn.*

quantity thus taken has been known to reach the large total of forty-three bushels, representing 2,752 sacks of wheat offered for sale and of a money value of £4,000, a very different state of things from the present aspect of affairs in the market House, where for many consecutive months not a single sack is brought and but a comparatively small quantity sold by sample. Yet with this large supply brought to market there was not enough to keep all the mills going as the demand was considerably in excess of these 2,700 sacks, and was made up by cargoes sent down from London.

'The sales or business of the Market were carried out...in the alleys or passages formed by the mode of pitching the corn.

'In many respects the old plan of bringing corn in bulk for sale had its advantages as well as disadvantages. The advantage was to the Miller, that he saw the whole bulk of his purchase instead of sample only. To the farmer the disadvantage was that he suffered the loss of the toll and if on the day his corn was brought he could not obtain a fair price, or what he considered a fair price, he had to take it back again or warehouse it until another market day came round, and this of course entailed considerable expense, and in the mean time the bulk was lessened frequently by pilferers, sometimes by accident and surely by rats.

'These disadvantages being so numerous, the plan of selling by sample at last superseded the old way, when it was found that as a rule bulks came in equal to sample and that convenient arrangements could be made for delivery without the inconvenient obligation of being at the Market with horses and men at a certain day and hour, these latter being thus freed and therefore at liberty to work on the farm.

'The decline of the corn market may be accounted for in many ways. Large tracts of the best land which formerly grew wheat are now used as Market Gardens and in other parts much that grew corn is now laid down as meadow and a considerable acreage has been built on; also a very large portion cut up into brickfields and more to form the lines of railway constructed in the district. Also upon the repeal of the

50. *Giles Hutson (1822-1904). Saddler and harnessmaker, author of the* Recollections of Uxbridge.

Corn Laws, steam having become almost universally used, many mills were started in London and worked by steam power and not by water power as our mills were.'

The growth of the sale of corn by sample was recognised by the Lords in Trust in 1859 when the Corn Exchange was instituted and the room above the Market House was altered to provide a place for business, but it was too late to halt the Market's decline. Some years previously the volume of corn passing through the Market House had severely damaged its structure. Mr Bassett, a corn dealer, had used the upper rooms to store his corn and on the night of 23 August 1851 the floor collapsed, injuring some men.

Corn was not the only commodity sold at the Thursday market. When the farmer brought his corn his wife would come too to buy household supplies, although by the 1880s most shops would deliver an order within quite a wide area. On market day the town's many shops were supplemented by street stalls selling every imaginable item. In addition the corner between St Margaret's and the Market House

51. *The Grapes Inn, 22 High Street.*

was set aside for a chicken and butter market and the corner opposite was used for the sale of vegetables.

In addition to the Market the fairs were held four times a year but as the Market declined so did the fairs, and they had ceased entirely by 1888. Luckily we have a very good description of the fair held on 29 September (known as the Statute Fair) in the 1850s. It was written by Thomas Strutt in his reminiscences of his childhood, the unpublished *Peregrinations of a Kiddy*. 'It is Statute Fair day, 29th September, and the streets are full of people, all flocking in from surrounding districts. The High Street on this side is lined with covered stalls, here and there with a caravan behind. On these stalls are displayed all kinds of articles; toys, whips, canes, whistles, trumpets, crackers etc., but several display Gilded cocks and hens, ducks, nuts and cakes, composed of Gingerbread. Stalls for nuts and walnuts. These extend from the Grapes Inn to below the Chequers by permission of the shopkeepers. The famous stall with its big round tin canisters with tray tops and its tastily set out shelves principally for Gingerbread nuts, is attended by the Misses King from Brentford. Their black hair in long Victorian ringlets on each side of the face. Their pitch on each occasion is in front of Mr John Rayner's the Chemist's shop.

'The Market House is lined with similar stalls, many of them for supplying the inner man of those who can manage it – winkles, crayfish, oyster, mussels and other shellfish, fried fish and potatoes, also black puddings, saveloys and such like delicacies.

'Greens and other toy stalls. The crowds of Farmers and their wives interviewing serving men and maidens who stood in groups for the yearly hiring. The labourers denoting their profession by placing in their hat wisps of hay for haycutters and binders; thatchers by bunches of straw; Horse Keepers by knots of whipcord, Ploughmen, Hedgers and Ditchers by some other sign. The General Fair proper is held in Heaborns Mead, a large open field on the right of Cowley Road opposite Prospect Terrace extending down to the river [Frays]. Generally Wombwells Menagerie, Moving Waxworks both with good outside bands of musicians. One or two circuses, swings and roundabouts, booths for giants, dwarfs, fat women, peep shows, noted boxers of the day – cocoanut shies, shooting galleries and so on, too diversified to mention, and crowds of people who all seem to enjoy it. In later years this part of the fair was held in the field surrounding the Wesleyan Chapel in New Windsor Street.'

The Statute Fair was the largest of the year; the first two fairs of the year, held in a large field along Harefield Road, were concerned primarily with the sale of cattle, sheep and horses.

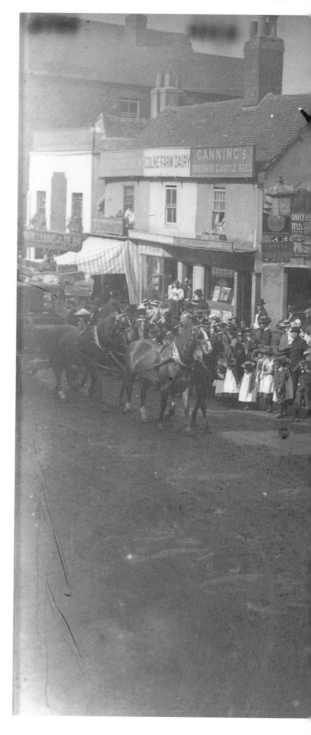

52. *Wombwell's Menagerie visiting Uxbridge, c1900.*

An Expanding Economy

NEW INDUSTRIES

Towards the end of the 18th century new industries were established in Uxbridge, counterbalancing the town's dependence on corn dealing and cattle fairs. One such was Thomas Lake's printing press, set up in 1770. Most surviving examples of the work of this firm date from the nineteenth century and include such items as sale catalogues, Redford and Riches' *History of Uxbridge* and the *Uxbridge Directory* until 1853; in 1828 Lake also published the *Uxbridge Note Book*, a series of pamphlets attacking the local administration.

Significantly, a bank was established in the town to cope with the increased trade. In 1791, two cousins from local brewing and milling families, Norton and Mercer, founded the Uxbridge Bank in premises at the west end of the High Street, now known as Old Bank House. Daniel Norton died in 1794, after which the bank was owned by the brothers, John and Nicholas Mercer; when they were declared bankrupt in 1805 the Bank was acquired by John Hull and reopened the following year trading as Hull, Smith and Norton, later Hull, Smith and Co.. Despite various changes in the partnership, particularly in the early nineteenth century, the bank remained firmly in the control of Uxbridge men until 1900, when it was absorbed into Barclays Bank.

THE GRAND JUNCTION CANAL

An important development in the economy of Uxbridge was the opening of the Grand Junction Canal. After a year's construction work the stretch from Uxbridge to Brentford on the Thames was opened on 3 November 1794, and celebrated with a waterborne procession along the canal. In his history of the Canal,

53. *Old Bank House, the premises of the Uxbridge Bank in 1791.*

54. *The Paddington Packet Boat; watercolour.*

55. *Fountain's Mill*

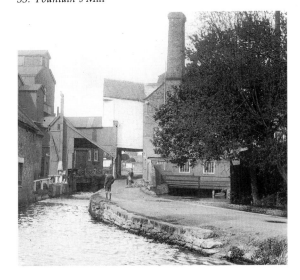

Alan Faulkner, quoting from the *Northampton Mercury*, describes the events thus: 'the opening of this part of the Canal was celebrated by a variety of mercantile persons of Brentford, Uxbridge, Rickmansworth and their vicinities, forming a large party, attended by a band of music, with flags and streamers, and several pieces of cannon, in a pleasure boat belonging to the Corporation of the City of London, preceding several barges laden with Timber, Coals and other Merchandize to Uxbridge'. It was not, however, until 1800 that the canal was built as far as Birmingham, thereby opening the way to the industrial midlands and the communications network of the north of England. For a short while there was also a regular passenger service between Paddington and Cowley, known as the Paddington Packet Boat, but this had ceased by 1810.

The canal even increased the importance of corn to Uxbridge. Several wharves and warehouses were built alongside the canal and by 1799 almost 10,000 tons of corn were carried between the Thames and Uxbridge each year, nearly all of which was milled in the town.

MILLS

At the height of Uxbridge's prosperity there were, according to Redford and Riches, thirteen mills working in the area. Three of these were in the town, the rest within a short distance along the Colne and Frays, and their wealthy owners, particularly the Hulls, the Fountains and the Mercers, were among

56. Fountains' Mill.

57. *A steam-driven delivery lorry for Fountains' Mill, c1900.*

58. *Rabb's Mill, c1880.*

the town's leading citizens. As Giles Hutson observed, even the large amount of corn passing through Uxbridge market was not enough to sustain these mills and extra supplies had to be brought in from London, usually by canal. The canal had made bulk transportation much cheaper and Frays Mill even had its own wharf. The mills were water powered and still dependent to an extent on the weather – too much rain was as bad as too little – but technological advances combined with the decline of the market itself led to a reduction in the number of mills in Uxbridge and by 1895 only four remained on the banks of the Frays.

GASWORKS

In 1806 an Act of Parliament was obtained to complete the paving of the town (begun in 1785) and its lighting. Both paving and lighting were confined to the High Street and ended at the town boundary at the top of Vine Street. The lights used were oil lamps, which gave out only a feeble glimmer. No lights at this time were very bright. In affluent houses expensive wax candles were used, but in shops and cottages oil lamps and tallow candles were usual. In the early years of the nineteenth century Messrs H. and D. Grainge experimented with gas lighting in their own workshops. This was so successful that they proposed

lighting the town between the King's Arms and the White Horse, at London prices, but the scheme came to nothing. In 1824 the British Gas Light Company applied to light the town, but were refused permission by the Lords in Trust and in about 1832 James Stacey, a private speculator, constructed a gas works behind the Dolphin public house on Uxbridge Moor. From here the High Street, shops and houses were supplied. At an inauguration ceremony held in the Boys' Schoolroom over the Market House there was a striking display of a large star formed by jets of gas. This supply arrangement continued until after 1854, when the newly formed Local Board of Health ordered that all public roads, and where possible alleyways, should be lighted. At first gas was not metered, but was charged at so much per light per year. Mr Stacey, who would walk the streets at night and complain if he found anyone with a light on stronger than he thought it ought to be, was eventually bought out by a few Uxbridge men and the company became known as the Uxbridge Old Gas Company. In 1854 John Hardy formed a new gas company, the Uxbridge and Hillingdon Gas Consumers Company, in competition and for a time gas was cheap, but the new company bought up the old in 1861 and was then able to charge what it liked.

59. London Street, Hillingdon End with gaslights; looking towards the Market House, c1880.

60. *Some of the last beer labels produced by Harman's in the 1950s.*

BREWERIES

Apart from the market, one of the staple industries of Uxbridge had always been brewing. There were four breweries in the town by 1851, and five by 1866. Harman's Brewery was in the High Street, at No. 180, and Heron's at No. 162; the Uxbridge Brewery was situated between Providence Chapel and the High Street, and this building later became the Uxbridge Steam Laundry, which itself was founded in 1882 and continued in business until 1962, when the premises were demolished during redevelopment. The Colne Brewery was behind Frays Mill. Both the last two breweries were owned by the Mercer family. The Windsor Street Brewery, belonging to Grimsdale and Wells, was in Chapel Street; this had closed by 1909. The last brewery to close was Harman's in 1964.

61. *(Above) Colne Brewery*

62. *(Right) Advertisement for the Uxbridge Brewery from* the Uxbridge Almanac *1867.*

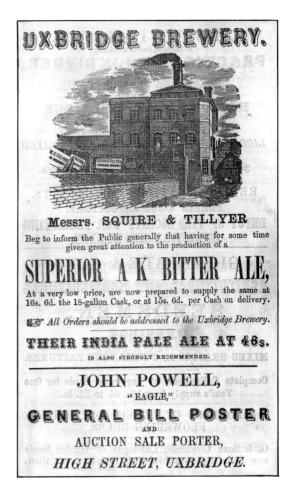

UXBRIDGE BREWERY.

Messrs. SQUIRE & TILLYER

Beg to inform the Public generally that having for some time given great attention to the production of a

SUPERIOR A K BITTER ALE,

At a very low price, are now prepared to supply the same at 16s. 6d. the 18-gallon Cask, or at 15s. 6d. per Cash on delivery.

☞ *All Orders should be addressed to the Uxbridge Brewery.*

THEIR INDIA PALE ALE AT 48s.

IS ALSO STRONGLY RECOMMENDED.

JOHN POWELL,

"EAGLE,"

GENERAL BILL POSTER

AND

AUCTION SALE PORTER,

HIGH STREET, UXBRIDGE.

63. Delivery van for the Steam Laundry, c1920.

64. The Uxbridge Steam Laundry, prior to demolition in 1962.

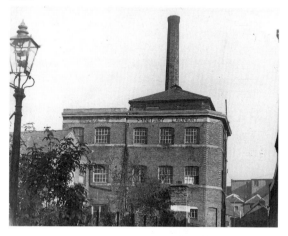

INNS

In 1853 there was the extraordinary total of fifty-four public houses in Uxbridge, of which twenty-four were in the High Street; but with the decline of the town and its market the number had reduced to forty-five in 1897, of which only seventeen were in the High Street, and there are now only four inns in the street. They were open all day, except on Sundays when, until the 1830s, they were open from early morning to Churchtime at eleven o'clock.

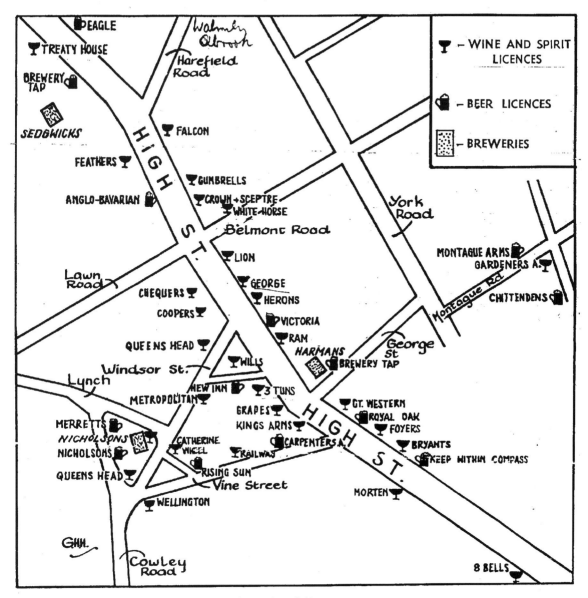

65. *Plan of the location of some of the inns and beerhouses in Uxbridge.*

66. *The Swan and Bottle between the Colne and the Canal. First recorded in 1761 it guarded the ford next to the High Bridge.*

67. *The Eight Bells next to St Andrew's Church. First recorded in 1747, demolished in 1972.*

68. The Falcon Inn, c1890. First recorded in 1747.

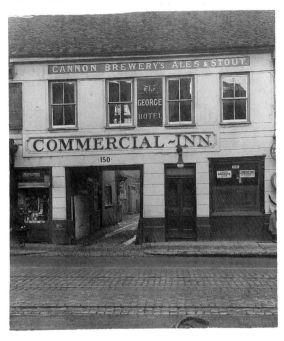

69. The George Hotel with its late nineteenth century front. First recorded in 1747, closed in 1960.

148. WASH MILL.

149. PUG MILL.

150. KICK AND STOCKBOARD.

151. STRIKE.

152. MOULD.

153. BARROW.

154. PALLET.

155. HACK BARROW.

156. PICK.

157. BRICKFIELD, MOULDER'S BENCH, KILN, &c.

158. SHOVEL.

159. METHOD OF LAYING HOLLOW BRICKS.

160. HOLLOW BRICK.

161. REED FLATS.

162. BARROW FOR CARRYING BAKED BRICKS.

70. *The brickmaker. From* Illustrations of Trades, *1860.*

BRICKMAKING

The opening of the Grand Junction Canal in 1796, with its cheap transport for heavy goods, provided the stimulus for the development of a new industry in the Uxbridge area. This was brickmaking. The area is very rich in suitable clay, but until the canal was built the transportation of bricks outside the local area was impossible. The first small brickfields to be worked were between Cowley and Yiewsley around 1815, but by 1818, according to Redford and Riches, several hundred men were employed in them. The industry grew rapidly. By 1856 over 240 acres in Hillingdon parish were being worked. It was a labour-intensive industry and its success led to a large influx of labourers, who were better paid than the agricultural workers. They were, according to Giles Hutson, often the worse for drink: '....many of that very rough class of workman or labourer, the brickmaker and navvy, made a practice of visiting Uxbridge on Saturday evenings. Money with these men at that time, at least during the summer, was plentiful, and their love of beer being great, they indulged largely and scenes of riot and violence were often to be witnessed'. The brickfields continued to expand until the 1880s, when supplies of brickearth began to run out and the industry was in decline by the turn of the century. The last brickworks closed at Stockley in 1935.

UXBRIDGE MOOR AND IRON WORKS

The Canal encouraged other industries. Warehouses and wharves sprang up on Uxbridge Moor and at the west end of town, and Uxbridge became the centre for the distribution of timber, slate and coal to the surrounding district. In the Uxbridge Moor area by the 1850s were a plate-glass mill, parchment works, oil mills and mustard mills as well as the gas works. The town also had some iron foundries, the oldest of which was Grainge, Rogers and Grainge who occupied premises off the High Street from about 1800. Stacey's Iron Works were built in George Street in the 1820s and employed about fifty men (George Street was named after one of James Stacey's sons). The factory closed down shortly before 1900. The Albert Iron Works opened in 1862 in Murray's Yard, behind the Falcon Inn. All these foundries made agricultural implements and domestic items.

Even so, Uxbridge did not become an industrial town, for despite the advantage of the canal the lack of a railway, at least at that formative stage, was a serious handicap.

71. Uxbridge High Street, c1880, showing the shop front for Stacey's Ironfoundry.

72. *Some products of Stacey's Ironfoundry.*

73. *George Stacey, c1850. Daguerrotype. (George was the son of James Stacey; George Street was named after him.)*

74. Garden scene at Mr Rich's villa at Cowley. Print of a painting by Hogarth.

Some Social Life

NOTABLE NEWCOMERS

By the middle of the eighteenth century Uxbridge had developed into a small social centre, though with the adjacency of London, it never became fashionable. Many chose the Uxbridge area for their country retreat as the surroundings of the town were still very rural. One such was John Rich, the proprietor of Covent Garden Theatre. He lived at Cowley Grove, the former home of the actor, Barton Booth, and among his visitors was William Hogarth, who painted a portrait of the family in the garden. On his death in 1761 Rich was buried at St John's church, Hillingdon.

Hillingdon House was rebuilt on the slopes of the hill near Hillingdon End by the Duke of Schomberg in 1717; it passed through several owners, including the Dowager Marchioness of Rockingham, who owned the house from 1785 until her death in 1805. Belmont, on Uxbridge Common, had been built at the end of the previous century and for many years the only access to the house was through the yard of the White Horse Inn. The present Belmont Road is the development of the driveway to the house.

75. Cowley Grove, shortly before demolition in 1964.

76. Hillingdon House, 1793.

77. *John Rich dressed as Harlequin*

78. *John Rich's tomb at·Hillingdon Church.*

79. *Robert Redman in the bar of the Catherine Wheel Inn. Drawn by William Mallam in 1824.*

AN ECCENTRIC NATIVE

Robert Redman, an unusual character, was born in Uxbridge. This is a description of him written in 1824, near the end of his life: 'This noted character is a native of Uxbridge, in Middlesex, was born in a house on Tattle Hill in that town, and for many years was a bricklayer. He was a man of great strength and foremost in every dangerous enterprise. He was not content with the homely food of his fellow workmen but would indulge himself, now and then, with a kitten, cat, or rat, which to his palate was "most delicious". He had so frequently eaten the dram glass after he had swallowed the gin that a late worthy landlady of the Chequers Inn would not allow him one, but gave him the liquor in a pewter measure. Half-pence, penny pieces, half-crowns and red hot tobacco pipes he has swallowed in abundance. He once challenged a famous jumper, Bob stipulated that he would choose his own ground and strange to tell he took the poor fellow to the top of the Church Steeple, stripped himself and jumped into the reservoir below with seven feet of water in it, which at that time supplied the town, and desired his adversary to follow him, but he declined and lost his Guinea, Bob having made the agreement for each to make one

jump only. He has pinned a bull more than once like a mastiff and once rode an unruly bull from Cranford to Hatton, where the poor animal laid down with him through fatigue. He had been drinking one evening rather freely and was returning to his lodgings on Tattle Hill when he says "I was seized by my collar and carried to the Mount on Uxbridge Moor, when I came to my senses I ran home as fast as I could and although there was a wooden bridge at Rockingham I ran through the River got home and went to bed. This fright I did not recover from for some weeks after". To this day he has not had a right idea how he got there – no doubt he was immoderately tipsy, strayed down to the Mount and went to sleep. He has always been a very fierce fellow, yet he is believed to have been strictly honest. He is now in the Workhouse at Uxbridge, is in good health, and was 90 years old last Michaelmas.'

EARLY CRICKET

Cricket is first mentioned as being played on Uxbridge Moor in 1735 and Uxbridge is the oldest club in Middlesex. Throughout the century games were played on Uxbridge Moor, including such matches as England *vs* Kent, which England won by an innings

80. The cricket ground at Cricketfield Road. Watercolour by Josiah Parlby, c1870.

Rules and Regulations

OF THE

UXBRIDGE AMATEUR CRICKET CLUB.

SUBSCRIPTIONS.

Honorary Members, Five Shillings ; Playing Members, Two Shillings and Sixpence.

CHAIRMAN AND PRESIDENT—Mr. G. EDEN.

1. That each member shall meet for practice on Uxbridge Common every Friday Evening, at a quarter before Seven o'clock, till the end of July ; and from August to the end of September, at half-past Six. Any of the said members not on the ground at the stated time shall be liable to a fine of Sixpence ; and if absent throughout the evening on any business whatever, or on the plea of bad weather, to be fined One Shilling, should the Umpire decide that the evening was favourable for play.

2. That honorary members are not subject to be fined for non-attendance, nor eligible to vote.

3. That no person be admitted in the club unless proposed and seconded by playing members, and carried by a majority of the members present.

4. That the secretary shall give notice to each member of any meeting, at which every playing member shall attend, or be fined Sixpence.

5. That all members residing more than one mile from the Common shall be exempt from the fines.

Committee,

Mr. H. AUSTIN,	Mr. J. MERCER, Jun.,
— H. GRIMSDALE,	— H. STEVENS, Jun.
— H. J. NORMAN, Jun.	— J. WILLIS.

Honorary Members,

Mr. Bedborough,	Mr. Hollick,
— Bird,	— T. Lake,
— F. Eden,	— H. Norton,
— Eves,	— Pullin,
— W. Gardiner,	— Treheru,
— Goodman,	*"R. Tate*

Playing Members,

Mr. H. Austin,	Mr. J. Haddock,
— H. S. Batt,	— S. Harris,
— W. W. Brownie,	— J. Mercer, Jun.,
— Chave,	— E. Mercer,
— H. Cosier,	— G. Noke,
— J. Croft,	— J. Norman, Jun.,
— G. Eden,	— W. Peake,
— J. Fountain,	— H. Stevens, Jun.
— E. Fountain,	— J. Stransom,
— T. Grimsdale,	— J. Willis.
— H. Grimsdale,	*— R. Murray*

Mr. J. STRANSOM, *Treasurer and Secretary.*

Mr. W. BUCKINGHAM, *Umpire.*

LAKE, PRINTER, UXBRIDGE.

81. *The rules of the Uxbridge Cricket Club, c1840.*

82. *Uxbridge Cricket Club, c1905, with some members of the Hampstead Cricket Club.*

83. *Some peaceful fishing on the tranquil River Colne, near Uxbridge. An early nineteenth-century print.*

and ten runs, in 1789. The club continued strong throughout the nineteenth century and is still flourishing. By the 1820s it had moved to Uxbridge Common and in 1858 moved again to a new ground in the centre of Uxbridge. This became known as Cricketfield Road and was the home of the club until 1971, when the development of the Civic Centre forced its removal to Park Road. One famous club member, from 1902 to 1914, was Bernard Bosanquet, who invented the googly. In the early days gambling on the result

was at least as important as the match itself, if not more so.

Prize fighting was also an extremely popular, if illegal, sport. In 1791 there was an attempt to stage a fight between the champion, Mendoza, and Ward on the Cricket Ground, Uxbridge Moor, but this was frustrated by the vigilance of the magistrates.

84. *Windsor Street about ten years after the railway took traffic away from the town. This is one of a pair of almost identical paintings made almost certainly by Thomas Gell, 'portrait artist and painter' for his son-in-law, James Blackwell. One of the paintings is still owned by the Blackwell family. The coach is the omnibus service from Uxbridge to West Drayton station, established by William Tollit in about 1840. Spencer Homewood, cornmiller, was the tenant of Upper Colham Mill, Uxbridge Moor, from 1832-1860. The furniture shop is the workshop of Badham & Bull, cabinet makers. In about 1849 Blackwell's took over this part of the building and extended their shop.*

A Body Blow to Uxbridge

The unthinkable happened in Uxbridge in the nineteenth century – the Market, around which the town had revolved, was reduced to a minor economic force. We have seen from Giles Hutson's remarks in a previous chapter (page 42), that there were various reasons for this, but the most devastating factor was the coming of the railways, or rather the decision of the Great Western Railway to avoid Uxbridge and route its line instead through West Drayton. This did enormous damage to trade in Uxbridge. While in 1836 the supremacy of Uxbridge in the area was acknowledged by the establishment of the *Uxbridge* Poor Law Union, in 1838, when the line opened, traffic immediately began to disappear from the main road and the town went into decline. The Market lost much of its business, some of the inns closed and by the end of the century Uxbridge had become merely the shopping centre for a small local district.

In the 1830s over eighty stage coaches a day passed through Uxbridge, as well as a vast number of private coaches, waggons and carts. Most were drawn by several horses, sometimes eight or more, and every inn yard in the town had large stables to accommodate them. The corn and hay to feed them came from local villages, such as Denham. Some small carts were pulled by dogs, but they were often cruelly treated, and in 1839 this was forbidden by law. Large herds of cattle and sheep were driven from grazing grounds in Wales and the Midlands to market in London. At times of the year the road was crowded with labourers walking from one district to another in search of work: hay time and harvest were particularly busy.

The railway changed all this and by the end of the century Uxbridge had become of minor importance, though the Cowley Road, leading to West Drayton, assumed a new importance, and between 1840 and 1842 William Tollit began an omnibus service linking Uxbridge with the new station.

A BRANCH LINE

As far as main line traffic was concerned, the damage was done. All that could be salvaged was a branch line to Uxbridge from West Drayton, which opened with a station at Vine Street in 1856: this proved so popular that the road itself had to be widened three years later. But it was not a particularly convenient line, being only single-track, and travellers to London had to change at West Drayton. Uxbridge never regained its position as a major market town and there were no further improvements in the town's communications until the next century.

85. *Vine Street, showing the station, c1890.*

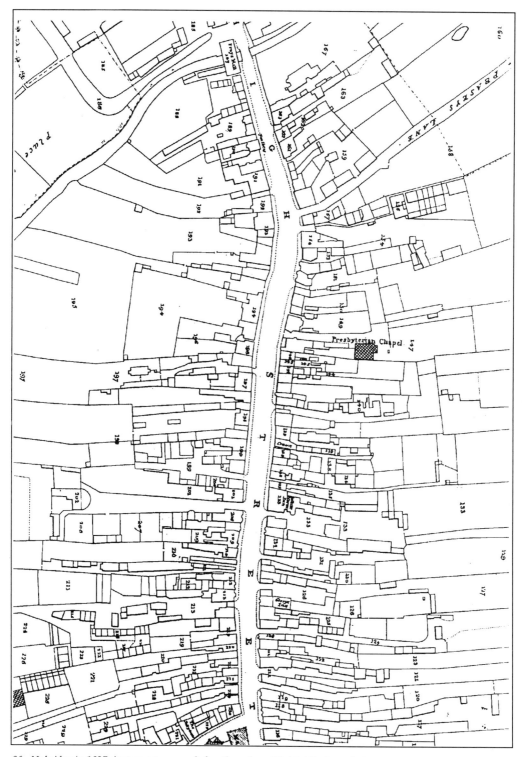

86. Uxbridge in 1827, just over ten years before the railway blighted the town fortunes.

87. *Nash's Yard, shortly before slum clearance in the 1920s.*

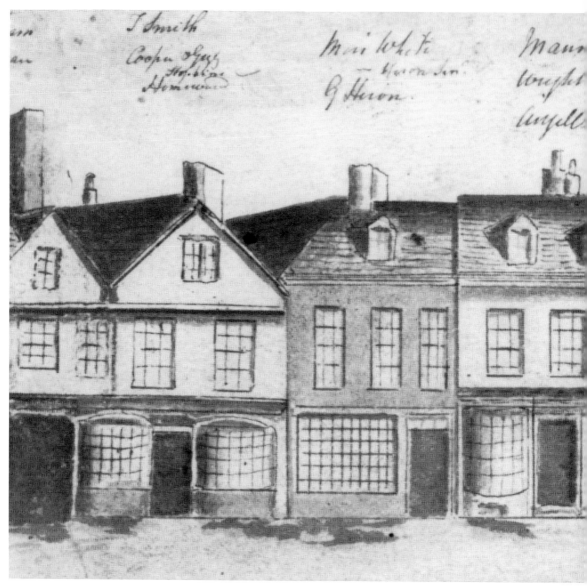

88. Part of the Uxbridge Panorama, drawn about 1800, before rebuilding and reconstruction of the High Street.

REBUILDING THE HIGH STREET

This disaster for Uxbridge came after a period of expansion. The population increased from 1,212 in 1782, to 2,111 in 1801, though only about thirty extra houses seem to have been built. Most of the old timber-framed buildings were either rebuilt or refronted so as to appear new, such as No. 119 High Street (at present a restaurant and formerly the Falcon Inn), which has an eighteenth-century brick front on the sixteenth-century timber frame.

At some time around 1800 William Burgiss painted the 'Uxbridge Panorama' on two long narrow strips of paper pasted on to linen, showing every house on both sides of the High Street, which justifies Redford and Riches' description of the town as having 'the appearance of being built in modern times'. This was the affluent face of Uxbridge: the hovels of the poor were hidden away down alleys behind the High Street, and as the population grew, the pressure on these yards became intense, so that by the nineteenth century the problem was acute.

More slums were added before 1831, but there was some better-class new housing outside the town, particularly along the London Road, near the entrance to Hillingdon House, after the fields of Hillingdon parish were enclosed in 1812. In the 1850s the presence of the Royal Elthorne Light Militia led to the development of the Greenway area.

But the speculative building caused some local disquiet. In the *Uxbridge Note Book* of 1828 the increase in crime and destitution was said to be caused by the rapid growth in the number of cottages.

'Instead of the poor being domiciled in the neighbouring country, where free air and small gardens preserve both their health and their morals they are now crowded into the town. The proximity of the market and the convenience of public houses, are frequently the temptations which allure the poor; while an exorbitant rate of interest for money employed in the erection of such buildings is the inducement with the owners...Cottages with two or three confined rooms and without even a back door or common sewer, may be seen by those willing to gain

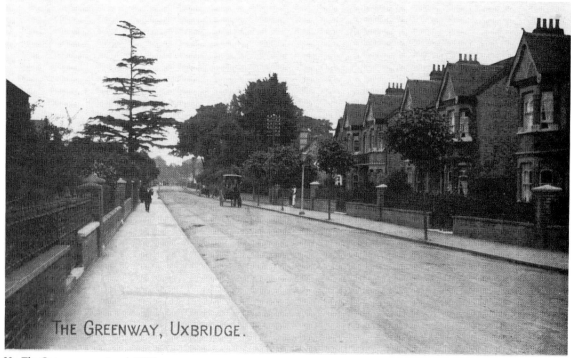

89. *The Greenway; postcard c1900*

information at the expense of their stomach.' However, this correspondent was more outraged that these cottages did not pay rates than at the squalor of their appearance.

Population had climbed again by the 1841 census, up to 3,219, but the extent of Uxbridge's loss of status is reflected in the fact that by 1901 the population was actually slightly less whereas around London generally it had risen substantially.

EXIT THE TRADERS
The decline took its toll on the well-established Uxbridge traders. Writing in the 1880s, Giles Hutson says that there was a complete change in the fifty years from 1830. 'A glance at the names over the shop fronts is to the old inhabitant more significant and more indicative of change than even the wholesale alterations in the fronts of shops and houses. Very few names are now to be found, the representatives of which were acting and energetic leaders of public local life and business then, almost all have passed away. The few, and there are not a score, are the names of descendants and are all that are to be recognised as having been to the front at that time. And not in any instance is the same person carrying on business now who did then; indeed, as far as can be ascertained, there is no one left who was in business in Uxbridge in 1830, so complete is the revolution which has been effected in that space of time.' That the nineteenth century was a period of change cannot be overstated and all aspects of life were affected.

90. (Above) *Brownie's rick cloth, sack and rope makers,*
140 High Street. Founded in 1813, closed 1935. Supplied
William IV, Victoria, Edward VII and George V.

91. (Right) *Uxbridge High Street c1850, by Trenchard.*

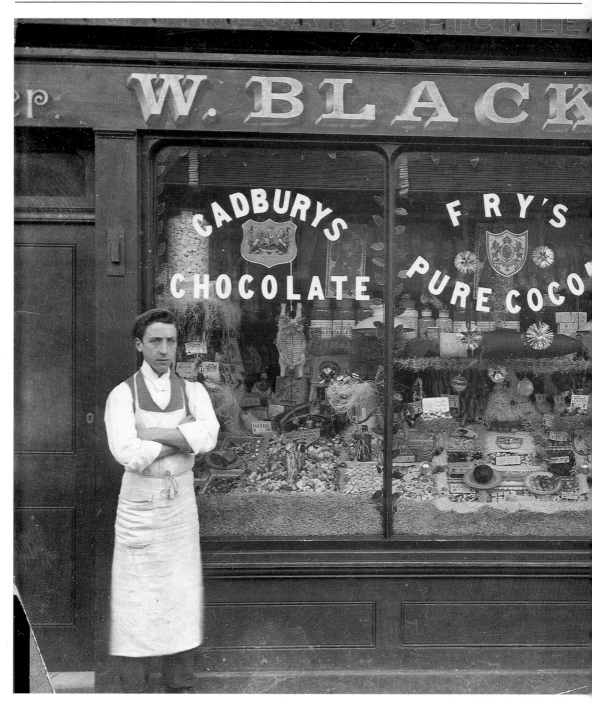

92. *Blackwell's confectioner's shop, 5 Windsor Street. Established c1840, closed 1929. This is the same shop shown in the painting of Windsor Street (Ill. 83) as it was refronted after 1850.*

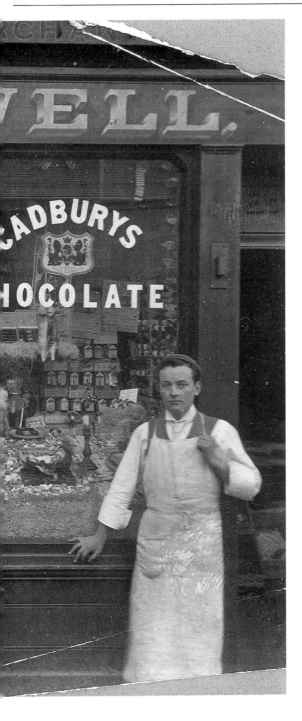

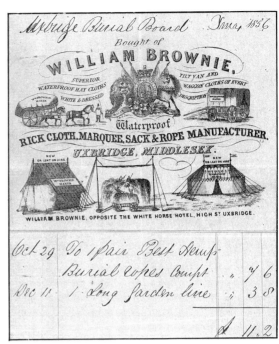

93. *A bill from Brownie's, 1856.*

94. *Transfer of business from Edwin Hedgcock, established 1845, to Carrick & Coles in 1868. The shop occupied a number of small premises on the corner of High Street and Windsor Street and was continually expanding. It was taken over by Messrs Suter's in 1924.*

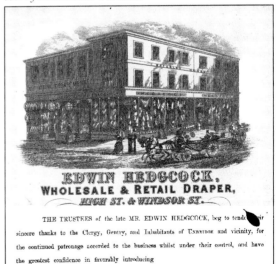

EDWIN HEDGCOCK,
WHOLESALE & RETAIL DRAPER,
HIGH ST. & WINDSOR ST.

THE TRUSTEES of the late MR. EDWIN HEDGCOCK, beg to tender their sincere thanks to the Clergy, Gentry, and Inhabitants of Uxbridge and vicinity, for the continued patronage accorded to the business whilst under their control, and have the greatest confidence in favorably introducing

MESSRS. CARRICK & COLES.

The established reputation as a man of business given them of the one, and their personal knowledge for so many years of the other, leave no room to doubt, that they will most fully and satisfactorily carry out all the requirements of this large and improving business.

95. Nicholls, pork butcher. Established c1833 at 127 High Street; later moved to 3 New Windsor Street. Closed 1969.

96. The rebuilt Randall's stores, Vine Street. Established in 1891, still going strong. The first purpose-built department store in Uxbridge.

An Unhealthy Town

A WATER SHORTAGE

At the beginning of the nineteenth century Uxbridge was a dirty, unhealthy town, lacking then even the piped water supply destroyed by the construction of the Grand Junction Canal. In 1800 the Lords in Trust ordered two deep wells to be sunk and others were dug privately or by subscription so that in the 1830s there were five public pumps working. Even so, this was inadequate for a town the size of Uxbridge and many of the poorer people were nearly two-thirds of a mile walk from the nearest fresh water.

The main streets of Uxbridge were kept swept and watered during this period by the inmates of the Workhouse, who used for this purpose small water trucks filled either at the town pumps or in the River Frays. This gave the false impression that Uxbridge was a clean town. According to Hutson: 'with all this presumed cleanliness, abominations existed not now to be dreamed of'. Down both sides of the High Street ran open square brick drains. By the 1880s these were used only for rainwater but in the 1830s they were the only method of drainage and sewage disposal. They took household waste, overflowing cesspools and other noxious sources. The yards leading from the High Street had only one open drain, down the centre of the yard, and these flowed into the main drain in the High Street. The Borough Ditch was also used as a cesspool. Attempts were made to deal with the sewage by having it collected by cart very morning, but this only added to the nuisance by leaving a bad smell in its wake for the rest of the day. To add to the smell, the drains flowed directly into the Frays, thus polluting it, and also many of the yard-dwellers kept pigs, often housing them in their cottages and allowing them to roam at will over the town. This was finally forbidden in 1840.

A MOUNTING DEATH RATE

The bad conditions of the cottages have already been noted. At the beginning of the nineteenth century there were no controls at all on building developments. The town was governed by eight men appointed by the Honor Court, a relic of medieval times; they consisted of two constables, four headboroughs and two ale-conners. Another official was the town crier. The Lords in Trust were concerned for the poor and in improvements to the town, but they had no interest in sanitation and it took serious outbreaks of cholera to change their minds.

There were also three unsavoury burial grounds in Uxbridge. Those attached to St Margaret's and to Providence Chapel were overfull and were believed

97. *The town pump outside St Margaret's church.*

98. *Constable's batons*

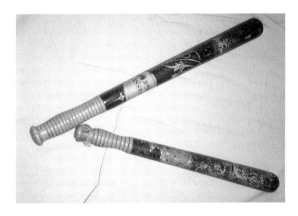

99. Frederick Gregory, last Town Crier of Uxbridge, 1892-1936.

100. Bell Yard about 1900.

Wanted Immediately
BY THE
RATEPAYERS
OF
Uxbridge,

A CLEVER FELLOW, to Report the doings of the Uxbridge "Board of Health!"

He must be a man of integrity, and with a nose 'cute enough to smell a rat.

He must possess a knowledge of Legal Points, bearing on the subject, well acquainted with Local Geography, and all the Mysterious Movements of "The Board" from its commencement; to be able to sift all the various little facts from the great heap of legal rubbish accumulated by the said "Board," and to lay before the Ratepayers of Uxbridge, a brief and concise report, whereby their judgments can arrive at some conclusion; *who* it is that is responsible for that series of insane blunders, which has brought down upon the Ratepayers of Uxbridge like a blasting blight, such oppressive and unbearable taxation.

The Reporters' services would be additionally useful, if he could also ascertain when the NEXT little Law Suit is coming on, and if, *when* the New Drainage reaches Yiewsley, it will stop there, or be carried on to the German Ocean.

N. B. No one need apply who cannot see through a Brick Wall, or glide through the Key Hole, as all Reporters are rigidly excluded from entering the Door.

Apply to Mr. G. Case, Central Vigilance Committee Room, Uxbridge.

101. Leaflet c.1860 complaining of the activities of the Uxbridge Local Board of Health.

to contaminate the water supply, and there was another by the Quaker Meeting House. In 1853, by Government order, the first two were closed on public health grounds and a Burial Board was formed which bought land off Kingston Lane for a new cemetery that opened in 1855. The first person to be buried there was George Yeoman, the town lamplighter.

The death rate was very high, particularly among young children; over one third died before their fifth birthday and the average adult life-expectancy was just over thirty-two years. It was cholera that finally spurred the townspeople into action. The disease first visited the town in 1831, brought by a tramp, but a cool autumn hampered the spread of the disease and Uxbridge was spared an epidemic. Cholera appeared again in 1849 and this time the epidemic, as in London, was very severe. It brought pressure for sanitary reform and the establishment of a Local Board of Health and in April 1849 Uxbridge was the first town in England to petition Parliament for an enquiry under the newly enacted Public Health Act. As a result William Ranger, superintending inspector to the General Board of Health, visited the town and made a report. He found that the worst conditions, as expected, were in the yards, where over a third of the population lived. Some yards, such as Chequers Yard, had no privy accommodation at all and were drained by open sewers. The improvements recom-

mended by Ranger included the construction of reservoirs on Uxbridge Common, which would enable every house to have a supply of clean water; existing privies were to be converted to water closets and many extra ones provided; tubular drains were to be used and problems arising from overcrowding and poor ventilation tackled.

In September 1849 the Uxbridge Local Board of Health held its first meeting. Its duties included 'the more effective paving and supplying with water, lighting, drainage and otherwise cleansing the town.' Power was vested in the Local Board to remove nuisances and to seize and have destroyed unwholesome meat, fish etc. exposed for public sale.

REFORM

But after this good beginning the reforms ran into trouble. There was much controversy about the jurisdiction of the Board and the expense of the proposals. The ratepayers felt that it was a fine idea in principle, but they should not have to pay. It was not until 1853 that the boundary was finally agreed upon and there were always grumbles at the cost of the work. The completion of the drainage and water system was made much more difficult when people refused to sell their land and the Board was forced to lay its pipes below public roads and footpaths; the reservoir on Uxbridge Common had to be built under the road as one man objected to the sale of sixty-five square feet of the common. The waterworks in Waterloo Road were in operation by 1854.

The 1848 Public Health Act provided for the appointment of a Medical Officer of Health, whose duties were to advise on preventive measures rather than treatment of the sick. The General Board of Health found it difficult to define those duties, so it was not until 1854 that Thomas James was appointed Medical Officer of Health for Uxbridge and he held the post until his death in 1883, when he was succeeded by William Rayner, the Uxbridge chemist.

The new water supply proved inadequate and was frequently turned off at night to conserve supplies. In 1889, to help the situation, the landlord of the Dolphin on Uxbridge Moor offered his deep well as an extra water source. The Rickmansworth Valley Water Company was formed in 1884, at first to serve only Rickmansworth, but in 1885 it extended as far as West Drayton and Hayes. In 1889 the Company laid its mains through the Uxbridge area, in return for which they supplied the town with water at a fixed rate.

The treatment and disposal of sewage was a problem. The sewage works on Uxbridge Moor discharged straight into the Colne, and there were frequent complaints from landowners and the Thames Conservancy that the river was seriously polluted. It was not until 1894 that anything was done to alter the method of treatment.

102. Uxbridge Cottage Hospital, Park Road, c1890.

By the end of the century there had been enormous improvements in the standard of living of even the poorest inhabitants of Uxbridge. Although slums still existed in the town the general level of housing was much cleaner and healthier; far fewer young children died and the average adult life-expectancy had increased to forty-three years. One factor in this was the opening of the Cottage Hospital in Park Road, funded by public subscription. Attitudes had also changed and local government controls over buildings, drainage and other matters were now expected.

CHANGES OF GOVERNMENT

In 1834 the Poor Law Amendment Act took the responsibility of caring for the poor away from the individual parishes, by adopting a system of grouping parishes into Unions. The Uxbridge Union covered much the same area as the present Hillingdon Borough. All the separate workhouses were closed and the paupers transferred to an enlarged Hillingdon Workhouse, which eventually formed the basis for the modern Hillingdon Hospital. In 1875 the Local Board became an Urban Sanitary Authority, with responsibility for the township of Uxbridge, and a Rural Sanitary Authority with responsibility for the rest of the area covered by the Uxbridge Poor Law Union. In 1894 the Uxbridge Urban District Council was formed; it took over the duties of all the previous boards, which were dissolved. On 1 April 1889, the newly-created Middlesex County Council took on responsibilities for county bridges, lunatic asylums, music and dancing licences and officers such as the coroner.

103.   *The Metropolitan Police at Uxbridge, c1900.*

Law and Order

POUNDING THE BEAT

Since the Middle Ages the town's two constables, latterly appointed by the Lords in Trust, had been responsible for keeping the peace, but by the nineteenth century they were inadequate for the task. In 1829 Sir Robert Peel set up the Metropolitan Police Force in London. This was so successful that other towns, including Uxbridge, decided to adopt a similar plan. According to Hutson there was a great deal of drunkenness and many unsolved burglaries in Uxbridge with which the constables and nightwatchmen could not cope. The two nightwatchmen, each equipped with a lantern and a heavy stick, walked the streets, calling out the time and the weather and often visiting public houses on the way and their noise gave thieves plenty of warning. They were seen as legitimate targets for drunken pranks. Hutson says: '...on one occasion the watchman, enclosed in his box, was laid with the door of the box downwards where he had ignominiously to remain until some person passed by who was willing to

104.   *Uxbridge Police Station, Windsor Street.*

assist him to get on his legs again. This watchbox was somewhat similar but not so substantial as the sentry boxes which are placed about government offices for the soldier on duty to retire to when the weather is bad, and was chained to the iron railings outside the Old Bank.'

With official law enforcement so bad residents formed themselves into societies to offer rewards and prosecute criminals, while several shopkeepers patrolled the streets themselves. The Uxbridge Volunteer Police force, formed in 1836, was housed in the recently vacated workhouse on Lynch Green. This consisted of one sergeant and three men under the control of the town Watch Committee.

In 1840 the area of the Metropolitan Police Force, established by Sir Robert Peel, was extended to include Uxbridge and this local force was disbanded. The Metropolitan Police station covered Uxbridge and Hillingdon and was situated on the corner of the Uxbridge Road and Kingston Lane; in 1871 a new station was built in Windsor Street and the Kingston Lane building closed.

A NOTABLE MURDER

Most of the cases dealt with by the Uxbridge Police were the routine ones of drunkenness and burglary. However, in 1869 there was a particularly gruesome murder, the facts of which hardly strained the detective skills of the force. In July, 32-year-old Frederick Redrup, known as Tom, the son of a local newsagent, and rather simple, met up with his friend, 23-year-old William Murray. They went drinking around the town and at about 6pm arrived at Murray's home in Smith's Buildings. Both were rather the worse for the drink and Murray's sister, Eliza Groom, found them both lying on the floor. She gave Redrup a pillow and left them. Ten minutes later she saw her brother leave, so went to check on Redrup and there found him him lying in a pool of blood, his throat cut almost severing the head from the body. Murray made his way to the Market House, where he announced "I've killed young Redrup. I cut his throat with a razor!" Murray was later sentenced to death, but this was commuted to life imprisonment. He died in prison in 1879, but no reason for the crime was ever recorded.

105. Smith's Buildings, the Lynch, shortly before demolition in the 1930s. Scene of the gruesome murder of Frederick Redrup in 1869.

FIRE!

The Local Board of Health was also responsible for the Uxbridge Volunteer Fire Brigade, formed in 1864, and based in a station in Windsor Street until 1909, when it moved to Cricketfield Road to make way for the new Post Office. In 1933 it moved again to the former Empire Electric Cinema in Vine Street. All the men were volunteers, rather like modern lifeboatmen; when the alarm sounded they would leave their businesses and run to the fire-station. They did not confine themselves to Uxbridge but were called upon by a very wide area around the town. Anyone who called out them out had to pay their expenses. The Volunteer Fire Brigade served the people of Uxbridge until the Second World War, when they were replaced by the full-time service of the London Fire Brigade.

106. (Above) The Uxbridge Volunteer Fire Brigade in 1880.

107. (Right) The fire station in Windsor Street.

108. School of Industry for Girls, from Redford and Riches' History of Uxbridge, *1818.*

A Place of Learning

NEW SCHOOLS

At the turn of the nineteenth century the two leading schools in Uxbridge were the Uxbridge Free School, founded in 1706 and supported by the Lords in Trust with the profits from the Market, and the Uxbridge School, a private venture founded in 1790. In 1809 the Free School was reorganised under the Lancasterian system, in which the older children helped to teach the younger. Then, in 1816, the Girls' School of Industry was founded, based on the previous free school for girls which had held its classes above the Market House. The girls were expected to pay for their education by their handicrafts, particularly sewing, the object being to turn out suitable servants. From 1817 a new building for the Girls' School was in George Yard, where about eighty girls attended. In addition there were several Dame schools where parents paid about fourpence a week for their children's rudimentary education. Poor children learnt little but how to read, write and do simple arithmetic, and it was not felt necessary to extend them any further.

By 1835 there were five day schools in Uxbridge: the British (formerly the Uxbridge Free School) School had 187 pupils, while 107 girls attended the School of Industry. The three others were small private affairs. There were also three girls' boarding schools as a counterpart to the boys' Uxbridge and Cave House Schools. In 1835 the British School and the School of Industry were reorganised and the inadequate boys' schoolroom over the Market House was replaced by new buildings in the Cowley Road. For some time the

profits from market tolls had been insufficient to support this school and in 1826 one penny a week, increased to twopence in 1833, was charged for each pupil. In 1836 the school received its first grant from the Government and despite financial difficulties throughout the century it survived until 1928, when the pupils were transferred to the Greenway County School. The Cowley Road premises then became the town's first full-time rate-supported library.

In 1820 Cave House School was founded. This private school catered mainly for the sons of local tradesmen and was situated in a substantial house at the west end of the High Street. In 1850 the then headmaster, Robert Wilkinson, moved the school to Totteridge Park in Hertfordshire, but the premises were taken over by another school with the same name. In 1878 the Cave House and Uxbridge Schools amalgamated but the reputations of both had declined and although it continued for some years it was not so successful and closed in 1900.

After 1835 several new schools were begun. New Windsor Street Infants' School opened in 1839, for between 140 and 170 pupils; in 1846 the Uxbridge Moor National School was erected on glebe land belonging to St John's Church, Uxbridge Moor. Unusually, though it was closely connected with the church, religious instruction was not compulsory. This school closed as recently as 1980. Also in 1846 the Uxbridge Moor Ragged School began, organised by the Waterloo Road Mission; by 1864 it occupied the Meeting House, with fifty-two pupils each paying twopence or a penny a week. All were taught reading and writing and the twelve oldest girls also learnt needlework. St Margaret's and St Andrew's National Schools were built within a few years of each other, in

1864 and 1869. St Margaret's infant department was added in 1869, by which time the school had 213 pupils. Many children had been bribed or otherwise persuaded to move from the rival British School, which owed no allegiance to the Church of England.

The 1870 Education Act made the provision of elementary education, if not attendance, compulsory. But there was no immediate consequence in Uxbridge because it was judged that the existing provision of voluntary and church schools was adequate and for the time being no Local School Board was set up to administer its own schools.

109. Advertisements for private schools in Uxbridge, from the 1875 Uxbridge directory.

CAVE HOUSE SCHOOL, UXBRIDGE.

In Union with ROYAL COLLEGE OF PRECEPTORS.

ESTABLISHED 1820.

Principals : MESSRS. HUNT AND GAYFER,

(Undergrad. of Trinity College, Dublin; Fellow of the Educational Institute of Scotland; and Associate of the Royal College of Preceptors).

IN this old-established School, Boys are quickly and efficiently prepared for Commercial pursuits, most Public Examinations, the Professions, Universities, and Public Schools.

At the Christmas Examination (1874) of Schools, held by the College of Preceptors, the Second Mathematical Prize offered by the Council was gained by a pupil from this School.

Great attention paid to backward or delicate boys, and everything done to promote the health and comfort of the pupils.

For prospectus, and all information, apply to either of the Principals.

15, MONTAGUE ROAD, UXBRIDGE.

MISS JENNINGS

RECEIVES UNDER HER CARE

YOUNG LADIES,

Between the Ages of 7 and 16,

AS BOARDERS AND DAY PUPILS,

To whose intellectual and moral culture her personal and careful attention is devoted.

A thorough knowledge of the ENGLISH LANGUAGE is imparted, with FRENCH and MUSIC.

Prospectus of Terms on Application.

---

110. St Margaret's School, the Lynch.

111. *St Margaret's Boys' School, 1916.*

112. *Miss Thonger's School, c1890.*

113. *John Bedford Leno (1824-1894). Born in Bell Yard, a leading member of the Chartist movement, a poet and an expert boot and shoemaker.*

114. *Gerald Massey (1828-1907). A member of the Chartist movement and a poet.*

RADICALS IN UXBRIDGE

The zest for self-improvement which so marks the nineteenth century saw the beginnings of evening education for working people and the establishment of societies dedicated to arts and sciences.

The earliest educational societies in the town were confined to the middle and upper classes. The oldest of these was the Uxbridge Book Society, consisting of about sixty members of the nobility, gentry and clergy of the area. Another was the Uxbridge Reading Society, formed in 1815. Both societies had sizeable libraries open only to their members. In 1836 the Literary and Scientific Institution was formed and these two societies merged with it.

Otherwise, the most important of the educational societies was the Uxbridge Young Men's Improvement Society. This was formed by two radical young men, John Bedford Leno and Gerald Massey, and others who wanted a literary society and reading room unconnected with any religion or political party. The Society was founded in 1845 with twenty-eight members; throughout its life membership averaged around eighty and it was still in existence in 1899. Classes and lectures were given in all sorts of subjects and discussion meetings were held; a good library was founded and several newspapers were subscribed to. The members also produced their own newspa-

pers, edited by Leno and Massey. These were *The Attempt*, *The Uxbridge Pioneer* and the *The Spirit of Freedom and Working Man's Vindicator*; they were all full of radical politics, the last most of all and it was nicknamed by one Uxbridge baker 'The Spirit of Mischief or Working Man's Window Breaker'.

John Bedford Leno was born in 1824 in Bell Yard in a poor but not destitute family and as a young boy he was apprenticed to the Uxbridge printer, William Lake. His early experiences led him to join the Chartist movement and he founded a branch in Uxbridge, and later, with Massey, began publishing radical pamphlets. They both left Uxbridge but still worked as printers in the radical cause, publishing books of poetry, a standard work on boot and shoe making and in 1892 his autobiography, *The Aftermath*. In this he declared that 'In my long life I have had but one strong desire, and that has been justice and freedom to all mankind'. He died in 1894 and is buried in Hillingdon Church.

His friend Gerald Massey was born in 1828, the son of a canal boatman at Tring. After a number of menial jobs in London he was apprenticed to Jones, the Uxbridge draper, where he made Leno's acquaintance, and then for a short while returned to London to make his reputation as a poet. He died in 1907.

115. *St John's Church, Uxbridge Moor. A pencil and wash drawing by E. Smith.*

116. *St Andrew's Church, Hillingdon End.*

New Parishes

The increased population of nineteenth-century Uxbridge stimulated the creation of new parishes and the parochial separation of Uxbridge from Hillingdon. St Margaret's became the parish church of Uxbridge in 1827, covering an area consistent with that of the town itself, but the rapid development of Uxbridge Moor led also to the building of St John the Evangelist in 1838. For the area known as Hillingdon End, the church of St Andrew's, built of Cowley bricks and designed by George Gilbert Scott, architect of the Midland Hotel at St Pancras Station, was opened in 1865 with its own parish.

The Evangelicals were also gathering strength. The Wesleyan Methodists opened a chapel in New Windsor Street in 1847, and from about 1851 there was a gospel mission organised in association with the Uxbridge Moor Ragged School in Waterloo Road. Another Methodist congregation was formed in 1864. Its first chapel, known as Burr Hall, was in Chiltern View Road, but services were held in several places until a permanent chapel was opened in Lawn Road in 1876. Other non-conformist sects which met in Uxbridge included the Catholic Apostolic Church in Montague Road from the 1850s until their chapel was destroyed by bombing in 1940. There was a small Baptist community in Uxbridge from the 1830s. Meetings were held in cottages in Bonsey's Yard and then in the Market House until a chapel, known as

117. *The Waterloo Road Mission in 1932.*

Montague Hall, was built in George Street in 1856, though it was a short-lived venture. In 1887 the Uxbridge Salvation Army Corps was formed, meeting first in premises in Bell Yard until 1899, when it moved to Montague Hall.

There was little Roman Catholic activity until 1891, when the church of Our Lady of Lourdes and St.Michael was formed under the influence of Fr. Wren of West Drayton.

There was also renovation and reconstruction of existing buildings. In 1818 the Quaker Meeting House was rebuilt, and this still stands. In about 1820 the tower of St Margaret's was completely rebuilt and at the same time the corner of the church was altered to widen Windsor Street; in 1872 the interior was thoroughly 'restored', when nearly all the windows were replaced, and in 1882 a vestry was built on the site of the old chicken market. In approximately 1850 Providence Chapel was refronted in the fashionable neoclassical style and the interior renovated in 1890. The Old Meeting House was substantially enlarged, whilst still retaining much of the original building, in 1883.

The Sunday School movement was very strong in Uxbridge. All the churches, to a greater or lesser extent, held their own Sunday School classes. Providence Chapel, which held classes twice a day both in Uxbridge and Uxbridge Moor, had over 200 pupils

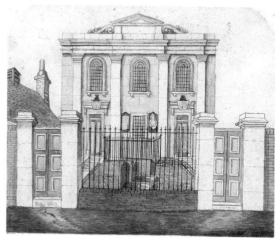

118. *The new front of Providence Chapel.*

registered in the 1870s. The teachers from all the churches would co-operate and held frequent meetings to discuss their work. In 1880, to celebrate the centenary of the founding of the Sunday School movement, 1,300 children from all the local non-conformist churches marched from Lawn Road to Hillingdon Park, preceded by the Hanwell Brass Band.

A Political Voice

At the beginning of the nineteenth century the electors of Uxbridge were still not separately represented in Parliament and shared a Member for the whole county of Middlesex. They also had to cast their vote in the county town of Brentford, where elections could last several days, during which time electors were bribed and entertained in the effort to capture their vote. But after the 1832 Reform Act Uxbridge was one of the centres at which polling could take place, in the boys' schoolroom over the Market House. This Act also widened the franchise, so that any male person who owned or rented a house or land worth more than £12 a year was entitled to vote.

Giles Hutson has left us a vivid description of an early nineteenth-century election, very different from the orderly affairs of today.

'At the upper end of the room the Sheriff with his clerks, agents and leading supporters of the candidates were stationed. On one side of the room a way was kept for the voters to pass up to give their votes at the head of the room, which having been done they returned by a corresponding way on the other side of the room, or which was frequently the case joined a body of onlookers assembled in the middle of the room.

'This gathering was mostly of a very unpolished character, and as the voters passed up the room they were cheered or hissed according to the view the assembly took of their political tendency. They were chaffed or groaned at according to the side these rowdies had ranged themselves on; and anyone who had outraged public opinion, or who was thought to have done so, or who from any cause was unpopular with the non-voter was assailed with the most unpleasant and leading questions as to his honesty, extraction, circumstances, wife, son, daughter or anything that was his or any other matter likely to be offensive.

'There were men with a coarse sort of ready wit who laid themselves out, or were employed by the agents of both political parties during the election and the names of George Bagley, Sam Powell and Mark Fisher will by some be recalled as the readiest, wittiest and most offensive of all.

'The interest taken in the County Elections immediately after the passing of the Reform Bill was very keen. The old inhabitant will remember that Lord Henly was put up on the Tory side but was not successful in ousting either George Byng or Mr. Joseph Hume, the other two candidates. After Lord Henly at another contested election Mr. Pownell was the chosen of the Tories and he also was unsuccessful but later Mr. Hume gave the greatest offence possible to the drink-selling people who had hitherto been his enthusiastic supporters by his advocacy of the movement which resulted in passing an Act forbidding the opening of public houses until 1 o'clock p.m.; an Act which perhaps more than any other ever passed led at once to a perceptible improvement in the habits of the lower class of working men – and in our own particular town to the stoppage of drunken riotous behaviour which had for so long scandalised the more steady-minded inhabitants. Again a Tory was put up, this time General Wood of Littleton, and as the publicans voted en-masse against Mr. Hume, the Tory candidate was returned. Shortly after, Mr. Byng, who had reached the distinction of being the oldest member of the House, died and his nephew was elected to the vacant seat which he held until he was removed to the House of Peers.'

The people of Uxbridge continued to vote for Members for Middlesex until 1884. In that year an Act gave Uxbridge its own Member of Parliament, and in the election of 1885 F.D. Dixon-Hartland, Conservative, was elected with 5093 votes, a majority of 2478 over his Liberal opponent. He was returned unopposed in the election of 1886 and also in 1895 and 1900. He won comfortably in the 1892 election, scraped in with a majority of 145 in 1906 and was still the Member for Uxbridge when he died in 1909. In the twenty years from 1885 to 1906 the electorate increased enormously, from 9902 to 15936. This was partly a result of increased population, but mostly a consequence of a widened franchise, enabling more men to vote.

119. Sir Frederick Dixon-Hartland MP (1838-1909), Member for Uxbridge 1885-1909.

Playing at Soldiers

THE CAVALRY

In 1797 the Uxbridge Yeomanry Cavalry was formed as a troop of volunteer cavalry in response to the threatened invasion of England by the French Revolutionary Army under Napoleon, though many people felt that the revolutionary fervour sweeping Europe might well affect the poorer classes here as well. As each Volunteer had to supply his own horse and equipment, only the wealthier members of the community participated, and it was commanded by Sir Christopher Baynes of Harefield Place, with Gregory Way, younger son of Benjamin Way of Denham Place, as Lieutenant, and Thomas Osborne, timber merchant of Uxbridge as Cornet. The troop trained and exercised on Uxbridge Moor, but was disbanded in 1801 after the fears of invasion and revolution had died down.

But the end of the Napoleonic Wars was followed by a severe economic depression thought by many of the poorer people to be caused by the introduction of machinery in manual activities. In the agricultural areas particularly there was great distress. Bands of starving farm labourers, inflamed by political agitators under the leadership of the fictitious Captain Swing, met together to destroy farm machinery, burn hay ricks and perpetrate other outrages. These riots occurred all over England and came as close to Uxbridge as Iver. In December 1830, labourers at Iver and Shredding Green, armed with cudgels, compelled householders to give them food, drink and money. Alarm spread to Uxbridge where the Uxbridge Yeomanry Cavalry was hastily reformed in case what was thought to be a rebellion spread.

The troop was never called on to put down a rising of agricultural workers and again in 1848, when they were put on the alert during the Chartist agitation, its ability and training were never tested.

The Corps trained for eight days each year, and for this the government paid 3s. 6d to each man, raised to

120. Uxbridge Yeomanry Cavalry uniform, 1879.

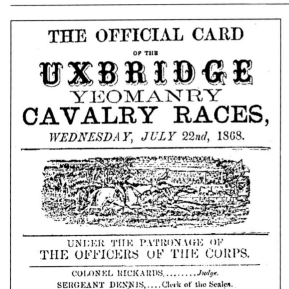

THE OFFICIAL CARD

OF THE

UXBRIDGE

YEOMANRY

CAVALRY RACES,

WEDNESDAY, JULY 22nd, 1868.

UNDER THE PATRONAGE OF

THE OFFICERS OF THE CORPS.

COLONEL RICKARDS........*Judge.*

SERGEANT DENNIS,....Clerk of the Scales.

121. Racecard for the Uxbridge Yeomanry Cavalry races, 1868.

7s 6d in 1840. Training, however, was more a social occasion than anything else. It began with a dinner to which the men invited the officers and ended with another where the officers invited the men. In between the men drilled on Uxbridge Common or on the estates belonging to the officers. On one occasion, during a drill on Uxbridge Common, the command was given to Charge!, but the officer forgot to order the men and horses to halt. Several soldiers jumped the ditch and hedge across Park Road and into Hillingdon House Park, but one horse got stuck in the ditch and several men fell off.

The troop was often called for escort duty on royal journeys. Its first attempt at this was not altogether successful. In 1834 the Uxbridge Yeomanry Cavalry escorted William IV on part of his journey between Windsor and Moor Park. The first part was accomplished successfully, but while the soldiers were awaiting the King at Moor Park they were liberally entertained and on the return journey, in high spirits, they got lost and ended up with the King stuck in a ploughed field. The Corps' last escort duty was performed in 1851 when it accompanied Queen Victoria from Windsor to Watford. Even this was not without incident, as lacking orders to the contrary, the Queen was taken on a roundabout route through Uxbridge so that as many people as possible could see her.

The Corps at first consisted of eighty mounted men and eighteen officers, although by 1839 it had fallen to sixty-seven men, of whom three were officers; in about 1843 a brass band was formed. Also at about this date races were instituted with the aim of improving the quality of the troops' horses on a race course

laid out in the grounds of Harefield Place, which was later moved to West Drayton. In 1871, as a result of the Franco-Prussian War, the Yeomanry Corps was enlarged and became known as the Middlesex Yeomanry Cavalry, with its headquarters still in Uxbridge. In 1877 the last training session was held in Uxbridge and from this date the local connection was slight. The descendants of the Uxbridge Yeomanry Cavalry, after many name changes, still exist as a signal corps in the Territorial Army.

THE INFANTRY

At the same time as the Yeomanry Cavalry was formed the Uxbridge Volunteer Infantry was raised. This was more popular with the local tradesmen and it did not require the possession of a good horse to join. Training drills were held on Uxbridge Common and rifle practice in gravel pits along Harefield Road under the leadership of Thomas Hurry Riches. The Corps was never called on for any military duty but often performed the service of protecting property after a fire. Mr Riches retired as commander after twenty years and was succeeded by Count Peter de Salis of Dawley Court. Soon after, interest in the Corps declined and it was disbanded.

THE MILITIA

During the 1830s the staff of the Royal West Middlesex Militia were stationed in Uxbridge. The depot consisted of non-commissioned officers who were trained to take charge of the regiment should it be called up. The men lived in Hillingdon End, opposite the entrance to the grounds of Hillingdon House. The Militia was raised by conscription – all males aged between eighteen and forty-five were eligible and the names were drawn by ballot. Those who could afford to would pay another man to take their place and Militia Clubs were formed in which members paid a small weekly sum and if called up the club would pay for their replacement. These clubs became redundant in 1848 when the Militia was reformed and voluntary enlistment became the method of recruitment.

In June 1853 the Royal Elthorne Light Infantry Militia was raised in Uxbridge and in 1881 was one of the regiments united to form the Duke of Cambridge's Own (Middlesex Regiment). During its short stay in Uxbridge the regiment made a lasting impression on the area. The troops were in barracks off the Greenway, in Enfield Place – the name probably came from the rifle used. Some of the houses in the Greenway were built to house the officers, and the street names Elthorne Road and Villiers Street both commemorate the regiment, as does the public house, the Militia Canteen.

122. *The Uxbridge Volunteer Infantry, c1860*

123. *The Militia Barracks, Enfield Place, shortly before demolition.*

Pastimes

HUNTING

There were still rustic recreations in Uxbridge at the beginning of the nineteenth century. Hunting in particular was popular. West Middlesex, with its newly enclosed fields and small hedges, was good fox-hunting country and the Old Berkeley Hunt met frequently in the area; stags were still chased over Uxbridge Common as late as 1826.

Hillingdon Fair in the 1830s still thrived. Giles Hutson tells how the fair, held on 16 May, attracted all the children and youths of the Uxbridge working classes. 'The amusement consists of the usual assortment of shows and so-called rural sports. These were climbing the greasy pole, dipping the head in water for oranges or into flour for money, or eating rolls which had been dipped into treacle and being suspended from a bar with a piece of string, the operator with his hands tied behind him took his stand under the roll bobbing and snapping at it until it was consumed, the prize being awarded to the one who demolished the delectable morsel in the shortest time.

'Sport of a kind very much more cruel was also provided at the fair. It is just fifty years ago [1830] since the last public badger baiting took place and this was at the fair. This sport was peculiarly acceptable to that contingent supplied by the brickfields; those people employed in that line being but a short remove from the savage, but they were not alone in their liking for cruelty for many persons of a much higher grade in life sought such scenes with avidity, and on this occasion the badger was drawn by a dog belonging to a very opulent and prominent person.'

ORGANISED SPORTS

The Uxbridge Cricket Club's games and the races organised by the Uxbridge Yeomanry Cavalry were popular sporting occasions. In 1870 the Uxbridge Amateur Football Club was founded, with home

124. Uxbridge Football Club, 1892-3.

125. Uxbridge Cycling Club, c1895.

matches on Uxbridge Common. An Uxbridge player, Hubert Heron, played for England several times and in 1876 he and his brother Frederick became the only two brothers ever to appear in an international side and an F.A. Cup winning side in the same season. By this time they were both playing for the Wanderers. In the 1888-89 season Uxbridge won the West Middlesex Cup, which they regained in 1891, 92 and 93, and in 1894 were founder members of the Southern League Division Two. Also in 1894 the team won the Middlesex Senior Cup, which they regained in 1896. In 1898 Uxbridge reached the finals of the F.A. Amateur Cup but they were narrowly defeated by Middlesbrough, who then turned professional. During all these successes the team remained firmly based in Uxbridge and nearly all the first team players had been born within half a mile of the Market House. Despite their playing record the club's expenses were not matched by income, and in 1899 the financial position was so bad it had to withdraw from the League and many players joined other clubs. Although the club soon revived it never attained its former status and remains today a local amateur club.

The Uxbridge Cycling club was founded in 1890 and organised weekly meetings, cycle races, sports and gymkhanas. In 1892 the Hillingdon Golf Club was formed and played on land that had been part of the Hillingdon House estate.

THE TOWN'S THEATRES

The earliest theatrical performances in the town were put on by travelling troupes which performed in local barns. The town's first permanent theatre was opened in 1820 by Mrs Burns and her sisters 'in an enclosed field belonging to Mr Allum near the bridge, Uxbridge.' This came to be known as the Treaty House Theatre. The repertoire included the play *Lovers' Vows*, which caused so much trouble in Jane Austen's *Mansfield Park*. Performances were often spoiled by the rowdy nature of the audience and Mrs.Burns and her sisters, according to their advertisements, were 'determined to keep the admissions to the amusements perfectly select; so that visitors may enjoy their entertainment perfectly free from the intrusion of improper company'. Visiting troupes also used this theatre, as well as large inn rooms, such as the Court Room at the George.

There were two improvised theatres in the town in the middle of the nineteenth century. The Windsor Street Theatre, near the site of the former Post Office, was in use in the 1830s and another site in Vine Street was used by travelling companies, first of all using tents; by 1849 this had developed into the Royal Prince of Wales Theatre (subsequently the Empire Electric Cinema). The town's only purpose-built theatre was the Theatre Royal in Chapel Street, opened in 1869 and in use until about 1914, mainly for the production of melodramas. The interior was sumptuously decorated in silver, gold and blue and held 365 people.

Much of the entertainment enjoyed by the people of Victorian Uxbridge was not professionally produced,

Mrs. Burn and Sisters

RESPECTFULLY INFORM THE LADIES OF

Uxbridge, and its Neighbourhood,

That they have erected a very Commodious Building in an enclosed Field belonging to Mr. ALLUM, near the Bridge, Uxbridge; where they purpose Teaching the,

POLITE ART OF ELOCUTION

SIX LESSONS .... Half-a-Guinea.

Also, Fashionable Dancing, Twelve Lessons for One Guinea.

Hours of Teaching, from Twelve to Four o'Clock each Day.

That the public may be enabled to judge of their capability, Mrs. B. and sisters intend converting the above Building, for the Amusement of the Inhabitants of Uxbridge, and its Vicinity, into a

Private Theatre,

Every Monday, Tuesday, Thursday, and Saturday

Mrs. BURN and Sisters are determined to keep the Admissions to this Amusement perfectly select; and although they will be proud to present Free Admissions to Box and Pit, to the respectable Inhabitants, it is indispensable that no Person can on any account be introduced, without first producing a Ticket for their Admission at the Gates.—The Teaching Room is erected in an enclosed Field, which is the private Property of Mr. ALLUM, who is resolved no encroachment shall be suffered upon the Premises: so that the Visitors may enjoy their Entertainment perfectly free from the intrusion of improper company.

NEAR THE BRIDGE UXBRIDGE

On MONDAY Evening next, July 17, 1820.

Will be performed, the admired Play of

LOVERS' VOWS,

The Characters by the following Amateur Performers:

Frederick, ... Mr. ALLEN, | Virdun, ... Mr. LAURENCE,
Baron Wildenhaim, ... Mr. SMITH, | Anhalt, ... Mr. PERRY,
Count Cassel, ... Mr. FORD, | Cottager, ... Mr JOHNSON,
Landlord, ... Mr. JONES,
Amelia Wildenheim, .. Miss ELDRED, —— Agatha Friburg, ... Mrs. ELDRED,
Cottager's Wife, ... Mrs. SMITH.

COMIC SINGING and DANCING.

126. *Playbill for the Treaty House Theatre 1820.*

128. *Playbill for the King's Arms Theatre, 1828.*

127. *The Theatre Royal, Chapel Street. After conversion to a warehouse in the 1930s.*

129. *The Public Rooms or Town Hall at the corner of Vine Street and High Street.*

but performed by amateurs. Though several of the large inns, particularly the George and the White Horse, had large assembly rooms where all sorts of meetings were held, the Public Rooms, or Town Hall, were built in 1837 at the top of Vine Street. These were used mainly for lectures, concerts and amateur dramatic performances, and by groups such as the

130. *Ellen Terry's cottage. This was also the brewery tap for Sedgwick's Colne Brewery. Ellen Terry changed the name to the Audrey Arms, after her dresser, and would often be found behind the bar serving.*

131. *The visit of 'General' Tom Thumb to the Town Hall in 1871.*

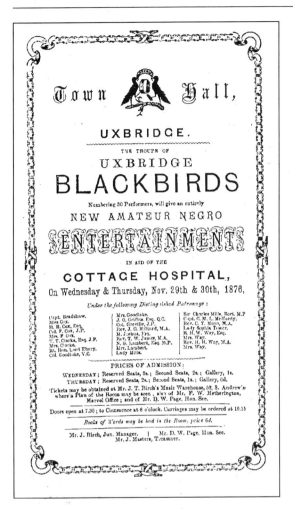

132. *Programme for the Uxbridge Blackbirds, 1878.*

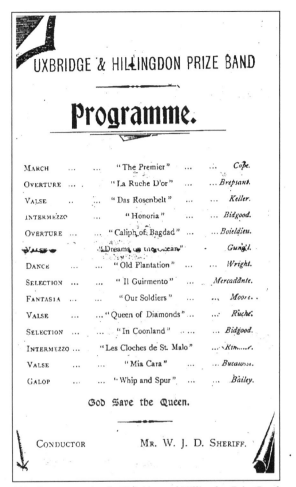

133. *Programme for the Uxbridge and Hillingdon Prize Band*

Uxbridge Blackbirds, which performed 'Negro' entertainments, and school orchestras and choirs. In December 1893, Gordon Craig, son of the actress Ellen Terry who had a weekend cottage in Uxbridge, made his first attempt at theatrical presentation at the Town Hall in an amateur production of Alfred de Musset's *No trifling with love.* He later became famous for his revolutionary ideas on stage design. The Town Hall was later converted to a cinema, The Savoy, and then a bingo hall.

THE LOCAL PRESS

The first local newspaper to appear regularly in the town was *Broadwater's Buckinghamshire Advertiser and Uxbridge Journal,* printed in Amersham and covering a wide area of Buckinghamshire and West Middlesex from 1840 onwards. From 1860 it was known simply as the *Buckinghamshire Advertiser* and was printed in the King's Arms Yard, Uxbridge. In 1880 John King founded the *Uxbridge Gazette.* W.J. Hutchings had acquired the *Advertiser* in 1903 and the two papers ran in competition until 1919 when the two firms amalgamated to form King & Hutchings, which still produces the *Buckinghamshire Advertiser* and the *Uxbridge Advertiser and Gazette* as well as many other local newspapers as part of the large Westminster Press company. In the 1870s the town had two other papers, the *Uxbridge Chronicle* and the *Uxbridge Marvel,* as well as the *Uxbridge Review* in the 1890s, but none of these survived long.

134. Dragonfield, St Andrew's, home of Cecil Sharp 1911-15.

A Revival

NEW RAILS TO UXBRIDGE

The beginning of the twentieth century found Uxbridge a sleepy backwater, on no main transport routes; although still a prosperous shopping centre, its influence as a market town had long since disappeared. It was a quiet place with a High Street still a mixture of private houses and locally owned shops, a town to which a person could retreat. People such as Cecil Sharp, the rediscoverer of English folk dance and music, lived at Dragonfield, St Andrew's, in Uxbridge to escape the business of London.

The new century was indelibly fixed by the death of Queen Victoria in 1901, for the event was seen to mark the end of a long era and the beginning of something quite different. The whole nation went into mourning. In Uxbridge, most of the shops were shuttered, flags flew at half mast, church bells tolled and the Uxbridge Prize Band played the 'Dead March' from *Saul*. The coronation of Edward VII was celebrated in usual Uxbridge fashion with parades and sports on the Common, and the same rituals were performed on the accession of George V eight years later.

But change for Uxbridge came not from any deaths in the royal family, but from the opening, in June 1904, of an extension to Uxbridge of the Metropolitan line from Harrow, with a terminus in Belmont Road. At last the town had a fast and frequent service to the City. In the same month the London United Tramways company extended its line from Southall to a terminus at the west end of Uxbridge High Street, and then in 1907 the Great Western opened its High Street station near the Treaty House, connecting to the main London-Wycombe line near Denham and also had plans to build a short line from here to its old station at Vine Street; to that end it purchased the necessary land.

Inevitably, after these improvements in transport, Uxbridge became more attractive for both businesses and people moving out of London. A large number of middle-class houses were built along the Cowley Road, Greenway, Harefield Road and Lawn Road, and around the edges of the old town centre. But even so Uxbridge remained a country town and still attracted visitors. On Sundays in summer and on bank holidays the town would be crowded with families intent on walking by the Colne, or having a picnic at the Swan and Bottle, possibly with tea later at one of the tea-shops.

135. *Old folks at a Jubilee tea, 1897.*

136. *Uxbridge celebrating the relief of Ladysmith, 1900.*

137. *Preparing the High Street for Queen Victoria's Golden Jubilee celebrations, 1887.*

WATER AND POWER

In 1906 the water supply to the town was improved by the erection of a castellated water tower on Uxbridge Common. The Uxbridge and District Electricity Supply Company set up business in Waterloo Road and by 1902 most of the town was connected, though even as late as 1912 houses were still being fitted with gas lighting.

138. *The water tower on Uxbridge Common, 1911.*

139. *The celebrations in the High Street to mark Queen Victoria's Golden Jubilee.*

140. *Official opening of the Harrow to Uxbridge Metropolitan Line Railway, June 1904.*

141. *Proclamation of George V, 10 May 1910, on the steps of the Market House.*

142. *Uxbridge High Street Station. A photograph of 1929, after the bridge over the High Street, intended to link with the line at Vine Street, had been removed.*

143. *A picnic at the Swan and Bottle, c1910. Note the tall masted sailing barge in the background moored in the canal dock at Eagle Wharf.*

144. *Uxbridge Metropolitan Railway Station*

145. *Alfred Button's wholesale grocers and provision merchants' depot with railway sidings at Belmont Road station.*

146. *Uxbridge by tram, by E. McKnight Kauffer. From a London Transport poster of 1924.*

THE COLNE RIVER AT
UXBRIDGE
BY TRAM

147. *The first tram in Uxbridge, June 1904.*

LOWE AND SHAWYER'S

New business came in the form of the Steel Barrel Company in premises in Rockingham Road, a company which was to prosper in the First World War. The grocery firm of Alfred Button opened a wholesale depot by the Belmont Road station, which has developed into the Budgen supermarket chain. There was also a flourishing nursery garden trade around Uxbridge. Before the First World War there were about six nurseries, the largest being Lowe and Shawyer's off Kingston Lane, begun in 1864 by Joseph Lowe in his back garden. In 1897 he owned several acres off Kingston Lane, specialising in growing roses and chrysanthemums. By 1914, when George Shawyer was a partner, the firm employed 300 – the largest employer in the district, and in the 1920s and 1930s the business still expanded until it became, with nearly 1000 employees, the largest cut-flower nursery in the country. Labour problems and cheap overseas competition caused the decline of the business, and it closed in 1958, but a reminder of this massive local undertaking is the presence of chyrsanthemums in the Uxbridge Borough coat of arms.

DIVERSIONS

The town's first cinema, Rockingham Hall, opened in the Lynch in 1909, and was followed a year later by the Empire Electric in Vine Street, opposite the station. The latter closed in 1932 and was converted for use as a fire station. In 1908 the town's first Boy Scout troop was formed in a garden shed in Chiltern View Road and in the same year there was great excitement in Uxbridge caused by the Olympic marathon competitors running through the town on their way from Windsor to London.

148. *Advertisement for the Steel Barrel Company.*

149. *Lowe & Shawyer's nurseries from the air, c1922. Hillingdon Hill and the RAF camp are at the top, Kingston Lane runs diagonally to the right.*

150. *The opening of Rockingham Hall Cinema, the Lynch, 1909.*

151. *The Empire Electric Cinema, Vine Street, after closure in 1932.*

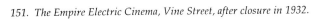

152. *George V inspecting machine gunners at the RFC, Uxbridge, 1918.*

153. *Supporters of the Uxbridge MP, Charles Mills, during the election of 1910.*

Between the Wars

CELEBRATING THE PEACE

When, in 1918, a notice appeared in the window of the *Uxbridge Gazette* announcing that an Armistice ending the Great War had been signed, the town went wild. Flags appeared, people cheered, the artillery guns at Hillingdon House fired and the church bells rang. Workmen and schoolchildren were given a half-day holiday and complete strangers kissed each other in the street. Even heavy rain could not dampen enthusiasm and the rejoicing went on all night, while the trains to London were packed with people going to join the festivities there.

The official celebrations were held in July 1919. Those in Uxbridge began with the ringing of church bells and included fancy-dress parades and sports on the Common with tea for the children, followed by dancing. The day ended with a torchlight procession round the town by demobilised soldiers and sailors, culminating in a bonfire and fireworks. The opportunity was also taken to christen the newly acquired motor fire-engine. In 1924, on Armistice Sunday, the memorial to the men of Uxbridge who fought and fell in the War was unveiled by the Dowager Lady Hil-

155. The Hon. Charles T. Mills, MP for Uxbridge 1910-15. The eldest son of Lord Hillingdon of Hillingdon Court, he was a popular local figure. He was killed fighting in France in 1915 and was replaced by his brother the Hon. A.R. Mills.

154. Unemployed social service centre, 1932.

156. Hunger marchers crossing the High Bridge, October 1932.

lingdon outside the St Andrew's Gate of the RAF camp at Hillingdon House; it was moved to the Old Burial Ground in the early 1970s to make room for road improvements. It was in fact a Peace Memorial, not a War Memorial, and unusually it has no names inscribed on it.

The Great War had some permanent effects on the neighbourhood. In May 1915 the executors of Col. Cox sold the Hillingdon House estate to the Cavendish Land Company, which then leased it to the government. It was used as a hospital and convalescent home for the Canadian army and then in 1917 the newly-formed Royal Flying Corps took the place for its Armaments and Gunnery School, so that the peace of Uxbridge was often shattered by the noise of guns used for practice. The RFC became the RAF the following year and the Hillingdon House estate was bought by the War Department; it was here that T.E. Lawrence, retreating from his notoriety as 'Lawrence of Arabia', trained for three months in 1922 under the name of

Aircraftman John Hume Ross. His book *The Mint* is a graphic account of the short time he spent there.

NEW BUSINESSES

The land the soldiers came back to was not the one they had been promised: it was not yet fit for heroes to live in and little had changed. The economy and many industries were in decline, the slums were still there, as were poverty and disease. But gradually new firms came to the area. The most important of these was the Bell Punch Company, housed in a disused mill on the Colne in 1919, which was to be one of the chief industrial employers in the town, manufacturing ticket-punching machines and other technical equipment. In 1921 Sanderson's opened their wallpaper and fabric printing factory on the Uxbridge border, and it is now their centre for worldwide distribution.

IMPROVEMENTS

The Uxbridge Urban District Council pursued a programme of improvements. It acquired the land no longer needed by the Great Western Railway after it had abandoned its scheme to link High Street and Vine Street stations, and laid it out as Rockingham Recreation Ground. Between 1919 and 1939 the Council built several housing estates, particularly on Uxbridge Moor and in the area between the Greenway and the London Road. During the 1930s there was large scale slum clearance in the High Street; most of the yards were demolished and their inhabitants rehoused on the new estates. The town acquired another recreation ground in 1926 when Mrs Kate Fassnidge gave a large part of her garden bordering the River Frays to the town as a memorial to her late husband.

In 1930 the Middlesex County Council took over the functions of the Board of Guardians, which had administered poor relief. Hillingdon Workhouse was immediately reorganised as the Uxbridge County Hospital, although it was generally known as Hillingdon Hospital and the name has stuck.

There were changes in the High Street. Old-established firms closed and were replaced by modern chain stores, such as Woolworth's. In 1921 the Town Hall closed and was rebuilt as the Savoy Cinema. In the same year the town's first bus services, operated by the Thames Valley Company, began on a route from High Wycombe to Uxbridge and a year later a bus garage was opened just over the border in Denham. Also in 1922 the town's first free public library opened in a house at the west end of the High Street, staffed entirely by volunteers; it moved, in 1930, to the former Cowley Road Boys' School as a full-time branch of Middlesex County Libraries.

There were other diversions. On Boxing Day 1931 the Regal Cinema opened in the High Street and later the Odeon was built at the west end of the High Street; in addition, the cinema in the RAF camp was avail-

157. *Moving into a new Council house, c1932.*

able to the public. In 1932 the Uxbridge Show, which had begun as a small horticultural event in 1909, was enlarged to include other events and except for a break during the Second World War, it has been an annual event (now called the Middlesex Show). The Frays and the Colne were used for swimming, though they were rather primitive, not very deep and also polluted, but in 1935 the Uxbridge Open Air Swimming Pool was opened on land belonging to the former Hillingdon House Farm.

Uxbridge, once the scene of numerous carts going through its High Street, was now invaded by cars. As a consequence the Western Avenue, most of which was opened in 1934, was built to divert traffic from the old Oxford Road, but traffic continued to go through the town until shortly before the last war when the link with the Oxford Road at Denham was completed.

There were important developments in public transport. The Piccadilly line reached Uxbridge in 1933 and as part of a slum clearance scheme Bell Yard was demolished to make way for a Metropolitan and Piccadilly line station, designed by Charles Holden, with an interior that includes an heraldic stained glass by Erwin Bossanyi. With its semi-circular forecourt facing the Market House it gave the town a focal point it had not had before. Trams in the town were replaced by trolleybuses in 1936, and a year later the old narrow High Bridge and canal bridge were rebuilt to take more traffic.

At the east end of the High Street the Uxbridge Urban District Council built new offices to replace the converted houses they were using. The new buildings, completed in 1939, included offices for both the Urban District and Middlesex County Council, and a library, museum and health clinic.

158. *Interior of the Regal cinema.*

159. *The old almshouses in the Lynch. These were demolished to make way for the town's first purpose-built post office, completed in 1909.*

160. *Opening of Uxbridge Library, 1930, by J.L. Garvin, editor of the* Observer.

161. *Aerial view of Uxbridge, 1933.*

162. *Bathing in the River Frays, June 1930. The river was much used until the open-air swimming pool was opened in 1935.*

163. *Plan sketch for the proposed Council Offices, designed by David Roberts of the Middlesex County Council, 1937. Only the left-hand portion was built.*

164. *Traffic congestion in the High Street in the 1930s.*

165. *Uxbridge Underground Station 1939.*

166. Miss Royle, headmistress, fitting gasmasks at Whitehall School.

Another Wartime

The emergency services had been preparing for the outbreak of a new war all through the summer of 1939 and the air-raid sirens were sounded as soon as it was declared. Cinemas and schools were closed immediately and unnecessarily, and both were reopened soon afterwards. A blackout was imposed, gas masks distributed, food rationing introduced and air-raid shelters built throughout the town; the main public shelter was in Laundry Yard, but 'Anderson' shelters were provided for people to erect in their own back gardens. As the war progressed 'Morrison' shelters were issued which could be used inside the house; one young boy found they were just right as a base for his model train set!

In August and September 1940 the area was bombed and two Uxbridge A.R.P. wardens, both Boy Scouts, were awarded the George Medal for rescuing people from damaged buildings. Houses in Rockingham Parade and Montague Road were hit, the Catholic Apostolic Church in Montague Road was demolished. In one incident several people were killed when hit by machine-gun bullets from an RAF plane chasing a German bomber.

This period saw the RAF camp at Hillingdon House at its busiest as Uxbridge was the control centre for No. 11 Fighter Group. Enemy aircraft were plotted from information sent from radar stations and observers in the south-east and fighter squadrons told where and when to intercept them. During the Battle of Britain Winston Churchill visited the operations room several times and it was here that he is reputed to have first said "Never in the field of human conflict was so much owed by so many to so few".

Though most development work in the town had stopped with the outbreak of war, two projects, however, were finished. The junction of Vine Street and the High Street was widened in 1940 and in 1941 St John's Isolation Hospital, founded in 1883, was extended. The builders of the hospital were congratulated on being able to finish the job under very difficult circumstances.

In 1941 a Food Advice Centre opened in the High Street to advise on how to make the rations stretch further and the food more palatable. A British Restaurant, run by the Urban District Council and the Ministry of Food, was opened in the old Waterloo Road Mission and aimed to provide a good meal for 10d (4p).

167. *Digging trenches on Uxbridge Common, 1939.*

A 'Dig for Victory' campaign encouraged people to grow their own vegetables and many new allotments were made available by the Council. There were appeals for salvage, such as old saucepans and iron railings which could be made into armaments. Funds were raised to help pay for munitions and in 1942 Uxbridge adopted *HMS Intrepid*, so that the town participated in paying towards its costs and comforts. The Home Guard, Air Raid Precautions and Auxiliary Fire Service were all staffed by volunteers, but as part of the emergency organisation the local fire brigades were centrally controlled under the London Fire Brigade and the Uxbridge Volunteer Fire Brigade ceased to exist as a separate entity in 1941.

168. Auxiliary ambulance personnel outside the County Buildings, 1940.

169. Uxbridge Home Guard machine gun section, 1941.

170 and 171. Street parties in Uxbridge.

Modern Times

BOROUGH STATUS

In the political transformation which followed the end of the Second World War, even Uxbridge, traditionally Conservative, elected Frank Beswick, its first Labour MP. At this election Uxbridge was joined by Ruislip and Northwood to form the constituency, but by 1950 Uxbridge was by itself sufficiently large and forward looking to have corporate ambitions. In 1951 the Uxbridge Urban District Council petitioned the government for borough status:

'Your petitioners believe that the granting of a Charter of Incorporation would tend to the great advantage of the District and to the promotion of its interests, by giving it a higher and more efficient form of Local Government and ensuring the stability of its institutions, by fostering public spirit and encouraging the more willing and efficient performance of public duties both by the inhabitants at large and by their elected representatives, by encouraging the car-

173. *Frank Beswick (1912-87), MP for Uxbridge 1945-59. Created a life peer in 1964.*

172. *Uxbridge Charter Day, 1955. The Duchess of Kent outside the Regal cinema.*

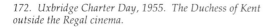

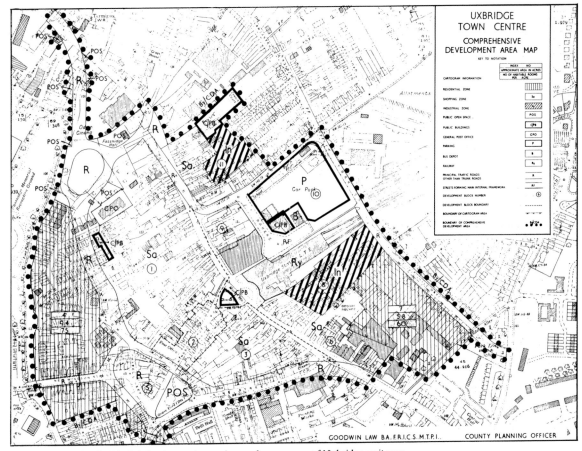

174. Proposals for the Block 1 development superimposed over a map of Uxbridge as it was.

rying out of measures for the further development of the District, and by giving to the District additional dignity, status and influence thereby enabling it to obtain that position among the Municipal Boroughs of the Kingdom to which its traditions, its growing wealth and advancement, large and increasing population and its enterprise, would appear justly to entitle it.'

The Council's ambition was realised in 1955 when the Duchess of Kent awarded Uxbridge its charter at a ceremony in the Regal cinema.

By the mid-1950s building schemes, such as Colham House, the government offices in Bakers Road, were progressing. There were also plans for redevelopment of the town centre, including the building of a new town hall. As properties in the area became vacant they remained so until that part of the town from Windsor Street to the High Bridge was virtually derelict. Businesses, such as Harman's Brewery and the Steel Barrel Company closed as did the old-established timber yard of Osborne Stevens – the site of this was redeveloped as the Highbridge Industrial Estate.

A NEW TOWN CENTRE

Detailed proposals for the new town centre were put forward in November 1963 but not approved until 1965. There was no doubt that the nature and function of Uxbridge had changed since the last war and that many buildings were obsolete. In particular, the old problem yards behind the High Street were semi-derelict and wasteful of land. It was decided to comprehensively redevelop the area within the old town boundaries. A relief road was designed to divert traffic from the High Street, which would then be pedestrianised this went through part of the old Colne Brewery and the Odeon cinema car park, with a roundabout to provide access to Harefield Road. This meant the demolition of Fassnidge Hall, an old people's day centre built only in 1960, and the destruction of much of the beautiful old gardens of the old Fassnidge home, the Cedars; houses in Basset Road, Lawn Road and the Lynch were taken down. The plan also involved the destruction, much lamented, of Cross Street, one of the most attractive parts of old Uxbridge.

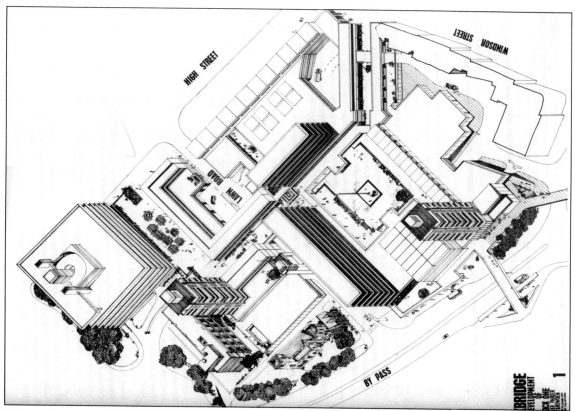

175. *Architect's view of the buildings in the Block 1 development.*

The original plan was to demolish most of Vine Street to widen the road, but when Vine Street station closed the line of the old railway tracks was used instead, cutting across the cricket field to rejoin the High Street at a new roundabout at the junction with Park Road, on the site of the Eight Bells public house.

In fact most of the existing buildings in the first stage of the scheme were taken down, on the basis that they were either too old or too obsolete to be worth saving. The yards were replaced by two squares, themselves lined with shops, one named after the old Chequers inn and the other called Market Square, where now a market is held on Thursday, Friday and Saturday. The first part of the shopping precinct, a grey concrete affair, was opened in late 1970. In all this many old Uxbridge shops disappeared, such as Kirby the ironmonger, Vernon Brown the seed and corn merchant and Rayner the chemist.

A NEW BOROUGH

The next stage in the transformation of Uxbridge began in 1973 with work on the site for the new Civic Centre in which it was intended to bring together all the borough's services. By this time London had been reorganised into larger units over an extended area. Thirty-two new boroughs had been created, obliterating the old Middlesex county as well as taking areas from Surrey, Kent, Hertfordshire and Essex. The old borough council of Uxbridge was merged with the urban district councils of Ruislip-Northwood, Hayes & Harlington, and Yiewsley & West Drayton to form Hillingdon, a name chosen after much discussion and dispute. In these new circumstances the redevelopment of Uxbridge as the town centre for Hillingdon became both a logical and desirable step.

The Civic Centre is architecturally different from the earlier part of the town redevelopment. It uses brick and tiles, instead of stark concrete, and is intended to harmonise with its suburban environment.

176. *Rayner's the chemists in the 1950s, one of the properties lost in the town redevelopment. It was established before 1830, and closed in 1962. The shop front is now in the Museum of London.*

LATER DEVELOPMENTS

Notable amongst the newer developments is Harman House, a glass-walled office block on the site of the old Harman brewery, opened in 1983. At the other end of the High Street the site of the Colne Brewery, for many years occupied by Hay-Lambert caramel manufacturers whose distinctive smell added much to the atmosphere of Uxbridge, has been replaced by another office block. The Odeon cinema also succumbed to offices, though a multi-screen cinema was incorporated in a new building. The entrance to Uxbridge over the canal bridge is now dominated by a large office block in the shape of a passenger liner, called The Quays.

Demolition of interesting old buildings was still proceeding even into the more recent era of conservation. The sixteenth-century timber-framed building of Burge and Gall in the High Street was taken down, though its timbers have been held in store for possible re-erection in future developments. More fortunate was the Regal cinema, a listed building for its art deco interior. The cinema closed in 1977, but it stood empty until recently reopened as a night club. In the triangle bounded by Windsor Street, High Street and Vine Street, another huge office block, Charter Place, and a new Central Library were opened in 1987.

Other landmarks which have either disappeared or radically changed include the Belmont Road station, which had been used by the Budgen grocery business – this was demolished to make way for a Sainsbury's store. In 1978 the Uxbridge Cottage Hospital was closed, ostensibly for renovation, but has now been sold for offices, and in 1984 the St John's Isolation Hospital in Kingston Lane was closed down. St Margaret's church was converted to community use, with some of it being let to local organisations, and the nave refurbished to provide a church for a diminished congregation.

177.   (Above) *The Civic Centre, 1991.*

178.   (Right) *The new Central Library, 1991. Designed by Frederick Gibberd and Partners. Opened September 1987.*

179. *Harman House, 1991.*

180. Brunel University.

BRUNEL UNIVERSITY

Uxbridge Technical College was opened by Anthony Crosland in 1966. Since then it has expanded to take in the former Townfield School site in Hayes, and has been renamed Uxbridge College.

The same year saw the first students arrive at the new Brunel University, which had developed from the Brunel College of Advanced Technology at Acton. With the closure of the Lowe and Shawyer's nursery, a large amount of land became available, and it is on this that Brunel is built.

SECOND THOUGHTS

Nearly thirty years after their inception the plans for transforming Uxbridge are near completion. However, attitudes have changed since those early days and wholesale demolition is not now approved of. In Uxbridge the whole of Windsor Street and the High Street from Windsor Street to Vine Street has been made a conservation area to try and preserve some part of the old atmosphere. The old Barclays Bank was gutted and rebuilt, but the facade kept, and there are plans to turn the old police station in Windsor Street into a pub and restaurant. At the same time it was appreciated just how unsuccessful the first wholescale development in the centre had been, and it has now been sold to the Prudential Assurance

181. Uxbridge Technical College.

Company which has completely refurbished it. The open squares were roofed over and the unsympathetic tall buildings refaced. The interior was revamped as the Pavilions Shopping Centre.

Today, there are few people living in the town centre. Though it is a bustling place by day, it is deserted at night – an empty shopping area surrounded by empty office buildings. Uxbridge has indeed changed.

182. *Artist's impression of the St George's shopping development*

183. *The Quays, 1991.*

184. *The Oxford Road crosses the site of Ellen Terry's cottage, with the office block above the Odeon in the background, 1991.*

185. *Metropolitan Police Station, Warwick Place, 1991.*

INDEX

Those pages marked with an asterisk denote illustrations